Ukraine's Euromaidan

Broadcasting through Information Wars with Hromadske Radio

MARTA DYCZOK

E-INTERNATIONAL RELATIONS PUBLISHING

E-International Relations
www.E-IR.info
Bristol, England
First published 2016

ISBN 978-1-910814-12-3 (paperback)
ISBN 978-1-910814-13-0 (e-book)

This book is published under a Creative Commons CC BY-NC 4.0 license. You are free to:

- **Share** — copy and redistribute the material in any medium or format
- **Adapt** — remix, transform, and build upon the material

Under the following terms:

- **Attribution** — You must give appropriate credit, provide a link to the license, and indicate if changes were made. You may do so in any reasonable manner, but not in any way that suggests the licensor endorses you or your use.
- **NonCommercial** — You may not use the material for commercial purposes.

Any of the above conditions can be waived if you get permission. Please contact info@e-ir.info for any such enquiries.

Other than the license terms noted above, there are no restrictions placed on the use and dissemination of this book for student learning materials / scholarly use.

Production: Michael Tang
Cover image: HappyCity via Depositphotos

A catalogue record for this book is available from the British Library

"Broadcasting history as it happens is the task that few journalists or historians can accomplish, unless they are at home in both professions and have an intimate knowledge not only of the scene they report on but also of the audience they talk to. Marta Dyczok brings all these qualities together in her radio reportages from Canada and Ukraine on the Euromaidan protests. Short, always to the point and easy to read, the reports demonstrate with unique clarity the global nature of today's politics and the power of the people on the street to change the course of history."

- Serhii Plokhy, Harvard University, Chair of Ukrainian History, author of *The Gates of Europe: A History of Ukraine*

"Marta Dyczok's ongoing research into how the control of media shaped political narratives in Ukraine has given her the qualifications and context to provide a rich commentary on the Euromaidan. Thus, this volume is an excellent example of how social science research can have direct relevance to current events. As the Research Dean of her Faculty during these years, I am proud to recognize Dyczok's engaged scholarship and to acknowledge her contributions in both the academic and public arenas."

- Andrew Nelson, Anthropology Department, University of Western Ontario

"The collection of reports in this book is an excellent contribution to the understanding of the events which followed one another in hectic succession from autumn 2013 to summer 2015. The reports written by Marta Dyczok for Hromadske Radio, the first truly independent radio in Ukraine during the last 3 years, give the reader a lively idea of the the dramatic facts and the discussions inside Ukraine, but also show the very different reactions in the countries which watched at the events from outside and tried to follow them. The reports are written in sober style, they privilege facts and description of the most significant events, but testify at the same time of the passion and professionalism the author puts in her work. Elegance and a subtle touch of irony make these reports an interesting reading for anybody interested in Ukrainian history and culture."

- Giovanna Brogi, Former Professor of Slavic Studies, University of Milan. President of the Italian Association of Ukrainian Studies

E-IR Open Access

Series Editor: Stephen McGlinchey

E-IR Open Access is a series of scholarly books presented in a format that preferences brevity and accessibility while retaining academic conventions. Each book is available in print and e-book, and is published under a Creative Commons CC BY-NC 4.0 license. As E-International Relations is committed to open access in the fullest sense, free electronic versions of all of our books, including this one, are available on the E-International Relations website.

Find out more at: http://www.e-ir.info/publications

Also available from E-International Relations

Environment, Climate Change and International Relations

System, Society and the World: Exploring the English School of International Relations (Second Edition)

Restoring Indigenous Self-Determination (new version)

Nations under God: The Geopolitics of Faith in the Twenty-first Century

Popular Culture and World Politics: Theories, Methods, Pedagogies

Ukraine and Russia: People, Politics, Propaganda and Perspectives

Caliphates and Islamic Global Politics (new version)

About the E-International Relations website

E-International Relations (www.E-IR.info) is the world's leading open access website for students and scholars of international politics. E-IR's daily publications feature expert articles, blogs, reviews and interviews – as well as a range of high quality student contributions. The website was established in November 2007 and now reaches over 200,000 unique visitors a month. E-IR is run by a registered non-profit organisation based in Bristol, England and staffed with an all-volunteer team of students and scholars.

Acknowledgements

My sincere thanks go out to Iryna Slavisnka, who first reached out to me from Hromadske Radio in the midst of the Euromaidan in January 2014, and to Andriy Kulykov, who then invited me to create these English language podcasts, produced them, and came up with the headlines. To all the listeners of the original podcasts for their positive feedback which encouraged me to share this with a wider audience. To Hromadske Radio for permission to reproduce the reports. To Ivan Malkovych, who assisted in the early phases of the book idea, and Agnieszka Pikulicka-Wilczewska, who suggested that I offer the manuscript to E-International Relations. To Ali Leon and Susan Viets for their feedback on the introduction and conclusion, to David Marples for the preface. And to Stephen McGlinchey for editing this book and making the publication possible.

Marta Dyczok is Associate Professor at the Departments of History and Political Science, Western University, Fellow at the University of Toronto's Munk School of Global Affairs, and Adjunct Professor at the National University of the Kyiv Mohyla Academy. She has published four books, including *Ukraine Twenty Years After Independence: Assessments, Perspectives, Challenges* (co-edited with Giovanna Brogi, 2015), *Media, Democracy and Freedom: The Post Communist Experience* (co-edited with Oxana Gaman-Golutvina, 2009), articles in various journals including *The Russian Journal of Communication* (2014), *Demokratizatsiya* (2014), and regularly provides media commentary. Her doctorate is from Oxford University and she researches mass media, memory, migration, and history.

Preface

The Historian as Public Analyst: The Case of Ukraine

DAVID R. MARPLES
UNIVERSITY OF ALBERTA

The current crisis in Ukraine has lasted over two years. Prior to that there were other outbreaks of mass protest against the ruling government, most notably in 1990, during the late Soviet period, and in late 2004 with the so-called Orange Revolution. In such circumstances it becomes difficult for scholars to determine their role, particularly if they are area experts. In the case of the Euromaidan, their situation is especially difficult because of the polarization of media opinion and the inflammatory nature of the events.

I have known Marta Dyczok for many years. In 2010, when I was a Visiting Scholar at the University of Toronto, we would have regular discussions at the Duke of York pub. From these emerged a major symposium we held, together with Rory Finnin, at the University of Cambridge on the 20th anniversary of Ukrainian independence.

Marta's career has combined media work with academic scholarship. More than any other person I can think of, she combines the two fields with relative ease. Her first book, published with Macmillan in 2000, looked at Ukrainian refugees during the Second World War. Almost simultaneously she published a concise study of contemporary Ukraine. But she has always continued to publish media articles and focus her work on the Ukrainian media. Moreover, she has the capacity and background to move within activist circles in the so-called Ukrainian Diaspora in Canada.

The events of the Euromaidan galvanized Ukrainians like no other event. Notable from the outset was a link between the Diaspora and the protesters in Kyiv and other cities, and perhaps especially in Western Ukraine, where the pro-European movement had advanced much further than in other regions. After Ukrainian independence, there was a veritable merging of many in the Diaspora with Ukrainian relatives and friends. In virtually every

Canadian city there were people starting businesses in Ukraine, moving there permanently or for long periods, as well as academic conferences and sponsored reform programs.

The importance of this development can hardly be exaggerated. For years the Diaspora prided itself on keeping the Ukrainian language and culture alive during the Soviet period. It also preserved its version of the memory of many historical events headed by the famine of 1932-33. Suddenly the "old enemy" no longer existed. Yet, in some ways the change was a mirage and the lengthy years of the presidency of Leonid Kuchma brought disillusionment appearing to move the country further away from Western-style democracy by its second term. What had really changed?

The Orange Revolution also brought disappointment in that the government of Viktor Yushchenko never really governed. It became mired in cabinet disputes and the president failed to address pressing problems. Ultimately he appointed as Prime Minister Viktor Yanukovych – the very figure against whom the uprising had been launched after fabrication of election results. Perhaps that is why the Euromaidan seemed so critical to the Diaspora. To some it represented a final break with the Soviet traditions after past failures and a move away from a newly revisionist Russia – which earlier had recognized independent Ukraine and the inviolability of its borders. Certainly in November 2013 that seemed to be the choice: the EU or Russia.

Let me add a caveat here. Because of her Ukrainian background, Marta has gone beyond the usual limits of the scholar. Most of us are far more reserved and distant. But, as noted above, there is a lengthy tradition of those of Ukrainian background living abroad expressing their commitment to the future of their ancestral homeland. I would acknowledge also that we disagree (sometimes strongly) on a number of issues, but that is fine. Good friends can live with such differences. I do accept though that she is sincere in her views.

The reports contained in this volume provide a highly readable and fascinating perspective of the phenomenon known as the Euromaidan – something that continues to evolve with no end point in sight. It has become much more than a local event, if indeed it ever could be described as such, because of its international involvement. Russia, the European Union, the United States and Canada play important roles. The Ukrainian conflict is an international issue. Ukraine can no longer be regarded as a post-Soviet state or one identified with Russkiy Mir. Since 1991 it has always remained on the periphery, or divorced completely, from the Russian-led structures that have emerged such as the Commonwealth of Independent States, the Eurasian Economic Union, and the Collective Security Treaty Organization. But, it may no longer be the same state as in 1991 and its final borders remain in dispute.

Scholars debate the nature of Euromaidan: is it a civil war or a war with Russia? Is it the start of a new Cold War? Should Ukraine join NATO to secure its borders? Will it bring Ukraine into Europe or end as a failed experiment with a weakened or permanently damaged state structure? Does it mark the failure of the post-Soviet order? As scholars we probably have to accept that we will not be able to analyze and comment with any certainty for another decade or two. That is why we are reliant on media analyses and reports? But who makes up the media?

Russian media have been active regarding the conflict, but the vast majority touts the line of the government which regards the Euromaidan as a coup carried out by extreme right-wing elements funded by the United States and others. Western media in Ukraine operate from a more objective stance but face a number of problems: access to leaders and activists, lack of language skills, lack of knowledge of the history of the state, and inability to fathom the plethora of parties and factions, as well as army groups, both official and volunteers.

Marta has no such dilemmas. She spends every summer in Ukraine, has lived in Kyiv for the past seven months, knows many of the main players on the Ukrainian side personally, and has appeared frequently on Ukrainian television and radio, as well as her media appearances in USA, Canada, the UK, Australia, Italy, Japan, and Hong Kong. Thus, she provides insights that are unique – not so much as an observer but as a participant. She can combine her academic expertise as an historian and political scientist, as well as her background in journalism and her lengthy association with Ukraine. And, that is why her voice should be heard.

Map of Ukraine

Introduction

They didn't say they were fighting an information war. The term was not yet in vogue. But when in the summer of 2013 a handful of Ukrainian journalists created Hromadske Radio (translated into English as Public Radio Ukraine)[1], that's precisely what they were doing. The independent radio project was a reaction against state and corporate censorship that was stifling free speech in Ukraine during Victor Yanukovych's presidency (2010-2014). 'Listen. Think.' became their motto.

Each journalist pitched in some money. They set up a website and began posting podcasts online. The internet was the one place that no one could interfere with their editorial freedom. And, they began to provide accurate and unbiased information to Ukrainians.

The Hromadske Radio pioneers likely had no idea how important and successful their project would become. In less than a year they were broadcasting live on national airwaves and reaching audiences in the eastern war-torn areas of the country on FM frequencies. Part of their success was due to their efforts, and part was good timing. A few months after their first podcast aired (on 23 August 2013) the Euromaidan protests erupted in Ukraine and spread through the country. But, accurate news and good analysis was still hard to find on Ukrainian radio. Riding the revolutionary wave, friends of the Hromadske Radio team offered them free airtime on their commercial music station, *Evropa Plus*. On 1 December 2013, they began their first live broadcasts, a show they called the "Euromaidan Marathon".

This helped the situation since at times it was difficult to get a clear picture of what was really going in Ukraine during the Euromaidan protests – both for people within the country and those watching from abroad. In large part this was due to the mixed reporting in Ukrainian and international media which began during the protests in late 2013, and continued through the annexation of Crimea and the hybrid war in Donbas that followed.

---

[1] See http://hromadskeradio.org/en

With a few exceptions, such as Hromadske Radio, the Ukrainian media continued to suffer from state and corporate censorship throughout the winter 2013-2014 protests. President Victor Yanukovych's information machine downplayed the size of unrest and depicted those taking to the streets as unemployed rabble rousers with fascist tendencies. Thus, Ukrainian audiences received a rather distorted image of events as they unfolded.

The Western media did not have many permanent correspondents in Ukraine. Reports often focused on the dramatic and stories were usually framed in simple terms: east vs west, Russia vs Europe, police vs protestors. And, Russia engaged in a sophisticated distortion campaign against Ukraine which permeated into international media as well as into Ukraine.

After Victor Yanukovych fled to Russia in February 2014, changes began in Ukraine's state owned media. Hromadske Radio was given two live hours on the national broadcaster Ukrainian Radio. At the time it was still owned by the state but had national broadcast reach. There was a lot to report on as Russia annexed Crimea and began a hybrid war against Ukraine.

Information warfare was a term that started being used around that time as it was an important component of all of these events. In February 2014 the Kremlin's disinformation campaign was broadened to distort the picture of what was really going on in Crimea, eastern Ukraine, and the rest of the country. Journalists and mass media outlets became both players and pawns in the war. New challenges arose over how to counter a powerful international disinformation campaign about Ukraine coming from Moscow.

During these events, the Hromadske Radio team grew and they gradually received more airtime. By January 2016 they were producing eight hours of live broadcasts daily – in addition to continuing their podcasts and developing a news service. This was a refreshing success story on Ukraine's media landscape.

But, the struggle for accurate information within and about the country has much deeper roots. The journalists who created Hromadske Radio were following in the footsteps of other Ukrainians who had been working to create independent media. Ukraine had been fighting an information war for decades. Access to sources and control over the collection and dissemination of information are issues that Ukrainian journalists and scholars have grappled with for generations.

Before Ukraine gained independence in 1991, some denied the very existence of a separate people called Ukrainians and considered them part of

Russia – little Russians, or younger brothers. During the Soviet era, a Ukrainian identity was acknowledged, but only within the context of a Soviet nation. The state owned and controlled all forms of media and there was no official room for alternative narratives.

A push for media change from below appeared during the *glasnost* years, when Mikhail Gorbachev started introducing reforms in the Soviet Union in 1985. Although there was an earlier tradition of independent minded journalists and intellectuals publishing samvydav (samizdat), they had a limited reach. Once Gorbachev began loosening restrictions on society, the trend of alternative media grew. Ukrainians, like others in the USSR, began producing many new unofficial media outlets. One of the earliest examples was *Postup,* created in L'viv in 1989.[2] The trend intensified once Soviet state censorship was officially lifted with the May 1990 *Law on the Press and Other Forms of Mass Information*.[3] But, for the most part, independent media remained small and self-funded.

After Ukraine gained independence in 1991 many new challenges appeared. Amidst a crumbling economy, leaders of an old nation that had achieved modern statehood struggled to build the state. Further, they had to deal with the world's third largest nuclear arsenal and the fallout of the 1986 Chornobyl disaster which had happened on their territory during the Soviet period. One important question was how to create a media environment which would provide impartial information to society.

When Ukraine broke away from the Soviet Union most of its media system remained in state hands. They inherited this from the Soviet era, when no private media was allowed. In the early 1990s there were many discussions about how to transform the former communist media landscapes. Conventional wisdom at the time, and advice coming from western advisers, was that media needed to be taken out of state hands and transferred into private ownership so that the media could act as a watchdog of the state. That's precisely what happened. Most of Ukraine's media outlets were privatized during Leonid Kuchma's first term as president in the mid-1990s. This was part of his larger privatization drive – and to some degree he viewed state owned media as just another asset. Most of the major media outlets

---

[2] See http://kipiani.org/samizdat/index.cgi?245. By coincidence, the newspaper's founder, Oleksandr Kryvenko, attempted to create Public Radio Ukraine in 2003.
[3] See Quigley, John, "Freedom of Expression in the Soviet Media," 11 Loy. L.A. Ent. L. Rev. 269 (1991). Available at: http://digitalcommons.lmu.edu/elr/vol11/iss2/1

were transferred into private hands, including two of the three existing TV channels that had national broadcast reach. Kuchma kept one TV channel, called UT1, in state hands, and one radio frequency, UR1. But overall, only about 10% of the media remained state owned.

However, state media outlets were privatized in a non-transparent manner. This created a pattern of interdependency between political and emerging corporate elites which continues to the present day. The first private broadcast licenses were given to groups that had close contacts with the president. Thus, in 1995 UT2 became Channel 1+1, owned by controversial businessman Vadim Rabinovych, film-maker Oleksandr Rodnians'kyi, and cosmetics heir Ronald Lauder – who was then building a media empire in Eastern Europe. UT3 was sold to Yevhen Pluzhnikov, a Kyiv businessman and key member of the then powerful Kyiv clan and SDPU(o) party. He brought in the State Property Fund and Russian TV Channel ORT as business partners and called his channel INTER. These two TV stations remain the leaders on Ukraine's television scene to the present, although they have changed ownership over time.[4]

Smaller TV channels also appeared throughout the 1990s. They were eventually bought up by other powerful businessmen (often called oligarchs) and grew into large media holdings. StarLightMedia was created by Kuchma's son-in-law Victor Pinchuk. Media Group Ukraine was set up by Rinat Akhmetov, Ukraine's richest man who once bankrolled Victor Yanukovych's Regions Party. And Channel 5 TV was created in 2003 by a man who would later become president, Petro Poroshenko.

Media and politics are always connected. Politicians need media to reach voters and attempt to shape public opinion, and media owners need government licenses to broadcast and publish. In today's globalized world close relations between political and corporate elites are the norm, where both direct and indirect pressures are used to control the media. Or as Gramsci would call it, establish a hegemony over the Habermasian public

---

[4] For an overview of early developments see, Dyczok, Marta, "*Threats to Free Speech in Ukraine: The Bigger Picture,*" in Giovanna Brogi, Marta Dyczok and Oxana Pachlovska (eds.) *Ukraine Twenty Years After Independence: Assessments, Perspectives, Challenges* (Rome: Aracne, 2015); Dyczok, Marta, "Ukraine's Changing Communicative Space: Destination Europe or the Soviet Past?" in Larissa M. L. Zaleska Onyshkevych and Maria G. Rewakowicz (eds.) *Contemporary Ukraine and Its European Cultural Identity* (New York, M. E. Sharpe, 2009): 375-394

sphere.[5] However, in Ukraine the media-politics relationship is complicated by the fact that media licenses were issued on the basis of political contacts. Both the new emerging businesspeople and politicians were engaged in corrupt practices that they wanted to conceal from the public. Thus, the media became an instrument in their power struggles amongst themselves and against the public interest.

During the later Kuchma years, censorship grew. One of the best known international examples is the disappearance of internet journalist Heorhii Gongadze in 2000. The president (Kuchma) was implicated in the case, although the real story of what happened is still not known. Growing censorship was one of the factors that fed public discontent that exploded in Ukraine's Orange Revolution in 2004 when massive winter street protests captured the world's attention.

A wave of optimism spread when the protests succeeded and Victor Yushchenko survived a poisoning attempt and was elected president. After he came to power, state censorship loosened and steps were made to convert the remaining state owned media into public broadcasters. Yet, within a year his popularity declined as political in-fighting in his camp intensified. He began lashing out at journalists who exposed his son's lavish lifestyle and failed to deliver on the promise of giving up control over the remaining state media assets.

Another disturbing trend in Ukraine's media during Yushchenko's presidency was that while state pressures on journalists noticeably decreased, corporate pressures increased. Media analyst Nataliya Ligacheva called this "corporate temnyky", a practice where media owners dictated what topics were to be included or excluded from the public sphere.

---

[5] Italian philosopher Antonio Gramsci wrote about hegemony, the political or cultural dominance or authority over others, in his Prison Notebooks. It was translated by Lynne Lawner and published in English as *Letters from Prison* (New York: Harper & Row, 1973). The public sphere is "an area in social life where individuals can come together to freely discuss and identify societal problems, and through that discussion influence political action." This term became widely used after German philosopher Jurgen Habermas published his seminal study, *Strukturwandel der Öffentlichkeit. Untersuchungen zu einer Kategorie der bürgerlichen Gesellschaft* in 1962. It was translated into English by Thomas Burger and Frederick Lawrence and published as *The Structural Transformation of the Public Sphere: An Inquiry into a Category of Bourgeois Society* (Cambridge: Polity Press, 1989).

After Victor Yanukovych was elected president in 2010, things got even worse. Corporate pressures remained and state pressures returned. By the summer of 2013, many analysts were writing that the situation with freedom of speech was worse than any time in Ukraine's modern history. And, that's when a number of grass roots media initiatives began to appear. They included Hromadske Radio, Hromadske.TV, Espresso.TV, Spil'no.TV. They all chose the internet as their platform. It was the one area that neither the state nor corporate world could control. And as it turned out, they were all well positioned to report on events in Ukraine when the Euromaidan protests erupted in November 2013.

I began receiving media calls in late 2013, when the Kyiv protests kept growing. Everybody wanted commentary, analysis. What was happening? What did it all mean? Where it was going? One call came from Ukraine. Iryna Slavinska phoned from Hromadske Radio in Kyiv. She interviewed me on how things looked from the Canadian perspective. Shortly afterwards, the radio project's co-founder Andriy Kulykov asked if I could do an English language report for them.

I agreed, prepared my first ever podcast, and sent it off. It aired on 3 February 2014. Over the following year and a half, I prepared 42 reports from Toronto, Mississauga, Kyiv, the Carpathian Mountains, Hlibivka village, London (Ontario), Sumy in eastern Ukraine, Edmonton, Odessa, and Ankara, Turkey.

These reports are collected in this book. They create a collage-like, kaleidoscopic chronicle of the events as I saw them from a variety of perspectives. From Canada, where I teach at Western University, from Ukraine, where I travel to conduct research, and from Turkey, where I attended the Second Crimean Tatar Congress.

THE REPORTS

3 February 2014 - 7 August 2015

Presented in chronological order and transcribed verbatim

Editor's note

Each report contains a link to the broadcast version. Readers of the paperback version of this book are encouraged to download a free e-book version from E-International Relations so they can more easily use the hyperlinks and listen to the reports. You can find
the book here: http://www.e-ir.info/publications

3 February 2014

Canadian Historian Watches History Being Made in Ukraine

https://soundcloud.com/hromadske-radio/canadian-historian-watches
https://soundcloud.com/hromadske-radio/marta_dyczok_23-01-2014

For weeks, I've been receiving calls from various media outlets to comment on what's happening in Ukraine and what's going to happen. I teach history and political science at Western University, I am a Fellow at the Petro Jacyk Program for the Study of Contemporary Ukraine at the University of Toronto and I travel to Ukraine regularly to conduct research on mass media and collective memory.

The images the Western media show from Ukraine often focus on the dramatic: clashes between protesters and riot police, attacks on journalists, deaths of protesters, high-level meetings and announcements by politicians, such as President Yanukovych travelling to Moscow, Prime Minister Azarov resigning, Canada introducing visa restrictions for key government officials responsible for violence or the latest Munich summit. The narratives are usually framed in rather simple terms. A struggle between Russia and Europe, East and West, police versus protesters. That's understandable in today's globalized 24/7 media environment, but does not always fully convey the complexity of what's going on.

Although I am following events closely, I have to confess that sometimes it's difficult to get a clear picture of events and their causes. In part, because there is so much information circulating, and in part, because many media sources in Ukraine, including social media, also focus on the dramatic. What is most disturbing is that violence is continuing and there seems to be no accountability by any government officials. I haven't seen any reports of investigations into the perpetrators of violence. Who was using live ammunition during the clashes on Hrushevs'ky Street on January 19th that resulted in a death of at least two protesters? Who is responsible for the kidnappings, the beatings, the torture, the deaths of activists and journalists?

Equally problematic is to answer when I'm asked of what exactly are the demands of the protesters. Despite all the positive energy that's been generated by the peaceful protest, the creativity, the clear flourishing of civil society, they do not seem to be speaking with one voice. It is clear that all those gathering in the streets of Kyiv and all over Ukraine are dissatisfied with their governing elite, that they would like to live in a country where rule of law, basic rights and freedoms are respected. What is less clear to me is how they envision this occurring in a short run, in a way that would enable them to feel satisfied that they have accomplished their goal and no longer have to stay in the cold on the barricades. It seems the only way out of the current crisis is through negotiation, but I am not clear who will be speaking to whom.

2 March 2014

UCC Organizes Protest in Toronto

http://hromadskeradio.org/2014/03/02/english-08/
https://soundcloud.com/hromadske-radio/ucc-organizes-protest-in

Thousands of people gathered on a busy street corner in the heart of Toronto on March 1st, the day Russian parliament authorized military intervention in Ukraine. A skyscraper stands where Bloor St. E. meets Church street. It houses the Russian Consulate. Politicians from all political parties, all levels of government, joined the rally, organized by the Ukrainian Canadian Congress, as did representatives from various communities, including Crimean Tatars, Poles, Lithuanians, and ordinary Torontonians.

They were protesting against Russian military intrusion into Ukraine. Liberal MP Chrystia Freeland said, "This is now a fight that has tremendous significance for the whole world."

Cars driving past honked their support for the crowd holding Ukrainian, Canadian, and other flags, and signs that read, "Putin, Hands off Ukraine", in big, bold letters. A nearby lamp post had a "Wanted" poster with deposed president Yanukovych's face. "Wanted for Mass Murder," it read.

As Crimean Tatar leader, Rustem Irsay finished saying "We are together with the Ukrainian people because we are Ukrainian," the crowd began chanting "Crimea is Ukraine."

This is the latest in a series of rallies organized by the Ukrainian community in Toronto. They began last November as soon as Ukrainians took to the streets in Kyiv.

Today's rally had wide media coverage. Many national and local national TV stations were reporting live on-site. Canada's Foreign Minister John Baird is in Ukraine at the moment. Another protest rally is planned in the same spot on Sunday 2 March.

10 March 2014

Reflections on Coverage by the Western Media

https://soundcloud.com/hromadske-radio/crisis-in-ukraine-what-is

Crisis in Ukraine: That's how many Western media outlets are framing the story. Facts are being reported, particularly stand offs, shots fired, clashes, statements by Russia's President Putin and Foreign Minister Lavrov, US President Obama, European leaders. OSCE observers being blocked from entering the peninsula. Occasionally Ukrainian leaders are referred to, sometimes even quoted.

On 3 March, AP reported, "Ukraine's mission to the United Nations is claiming that 16,000 Russian troops have been deployed in the strategic Crimea region, while Russia's UN ambassador told the council Monday that Ukraine's fugitive president requested troops."

That same day in a live broadcast, CNN anchor Wolf Blitzer repeated a claim by Russia's United Nations Ambassador, Vitaly Churkin that Nazi sympathizers have taken power in Western Ukraine. His colleague CNN International Correspondent, Christiane Amanpour, jumped in and said, "You've got to be really careful putting that across as a fact."

All major international media reported on rival pro-unity and pro-Russian rallies held on 9 March, especially the ones where violence broke out. Few noted that a day earlier, on International Women's Day, around 20,000 Crimean women held mass peace rallies throughout the peninsula. Or that Ukrainian Jewish organizations had written an open letter to Putin, saying, "The Russian-speaking citizens of Ukraine are not being humiliated or discriminated against; their civil rights have not been limited."

Russian Foreign Minister Sergei Lavrov said on 8 March the crisis in Ukraine was "created artificially for purely geopolitical reasons... We didn't create this crisis." 200 years ago, Taras Shevchenko, Ukraine's Shakespeare, was born. In 1845 he wrote, "They're saying, you see, that all of it, Was always ours" ("Кажуть, бачиш, що все то те, Таки й було наше").

17 March 2014

Peace March in Support Of Ukraine: More Flags than Ever Before

http://hromadskeradio.org/2014/03/17/english-11/
https://soundcloud.com/hromadske-radio/peace-march-in-support-of

Canada's Prime Minister Stephen Harper denounced what he said was a "so-called referendum" held in Crimea. "Its results are a reflection of nothing more than Russian military control," he said in a statement. As on every Sunday since the Euromaidan began, a rally in solidarity with Ukraine was held in Toronto on March 16.

In churches all over Toronto, Ukrainians were praying harder than usual this Sunday. Praying for peace and unity in Ukraine.

In the afternoon they gathered at Yonge Dundas Square, the heart of the city's commercial core, for a peace march.

It's difficult to give a good estimate of numbers, hundreds, perhaps thousands. Some arrived by public transport. I spotted many blue and yellow flags in the TTC on my way there. Others came by car, sporting blue and yellow flags, the Toronto AutoMaidan, honking as they drove alongside those who were walking, chanting the now familiar, "Hands off Ukraine, Putin." Still others joined along the way. My phone rang, a friend calling, "Where are you now, which consulate is next?"

The peace march went past a number of diplomatic missions located in downtown Toronto. In front of the US Consulate, there were both thanks and calls for sanctions. "We would also like to thank the US for what they're doing and their brave demands for sanctions against Moscow."

Ukrainians in Toronto have been gathering every Sunday since the Euromaidan protests began in Kyiv in November. They have been joined by others. This week there were more diverse flags than ever before. Nestine Eniega brought greetings from Toronto's Baltic communities. "On behalf of the Latvian National Federation of Canada, Latvian National Youth Association, and the Baltic Federation, we bring you sincere greetings from our community."

As the crowd headed for the next stop, the British Consulate, I spotted a sign that read, "Canadian Friends of Tibet." A man walking underneath it turned out to be Kunga Tsiring, co-chair of the society. He explained why he joined the peace march, that Tibetans had a similar experience in the past. "I'm here as solidarity and moral support to the people of Ukraine, and at the same time I strongly condemn the Russian military invasion of Crimea. Tibet was occupied by China after forceful signing with the representative of the Tibetan government." He added, "Tibetans have become second class citizens in our own homeland."

The next stop was the German Consulate, after which the peace march headed for the Russian Consulate. There it became so loud I could hardly hear the person at the other end of my phone.

23 March 2014

"In Ukraine, where he should be"

https://soundcloud.com/hromadske-radio/in-ukraine-where-he-should-be

With everything else going on in Ukraine, it's hardly surprising that Canadian Prime Minister Stephen Harper's visit to Kyiv this weekend, was not the top story. Ukraine's acting Prime Minister, Arseniy Yatseniuk, met with his Canadian counterpart, despite the country being invaded, Russian troops storming the Belbeck air base in Crimea, and countless other crises.

Harper is the first G7 leader to visit Ukraine since Russia invaded. He made a lengthy detour on his way to the upcoming G7 meeting in The Hague, to show Canada's support for Ukraine. Canada was the first country to impose sanctions against Russia when it invaded Crimea, a step that was followed by the more powerful US and EU.

Canada is not a great power, but neither is it insignificant. In 1991 it was the first western country to recognize Ukraine's independence, a move followed by others.

In 1956 former Canadian Prime Minister Lester B. Pearson came up with the idea of peacekeeping as a way out of the Suez Crisis. Now, as the international community stands at a precipice, with few effective mechanisms to stop or reverse military aggression by a major power that possesses nuclear weapons, perhaps a contemporary Canadian will come up with a solution to peacefully resolve the 2014 Ukraine Crisis.

Curious how much the average Canadian was following the situation in Ukraine, when finished my Saturday shopping, I casually asked the check-out clerk, "Do you know where Prime Minister Harper is today?" He answered immediately, "In Ukraine, where he should be. We need to offer them our support." As I finished paying he added, "I'm glad we introduced sanctions against Russia, even if it hurts us and the global economy. We can't let Putin get away with it."

Earlier in the day I'd read a report on the Kremlin-controlled Russia Today. A protest against the spread of fascism in Ukraine was planned in Toronto for Sunday, the day that Toronto Ukrainians regularly gather to support democracy in Ukraine. The Russia Today report also stated that the meeting would condemn Prime Minister Harper's visit to Ukraine, but did not say where the meeting would be held. I'll do my best to find out and go, to see who gathers, and what they have to say.

What Ukraine asked Canada is to re-open discussions about a free trade zone, a conversation that stalled after 2012. As Harper was departing Kyiv for the G7 summit, a meeting that Russia was pointedly uninvited to, Yatseniuk said, "If there's an empty seat at the G8, Ukraine would be happy to take it up."

25 March 2014

Russia Slaps Sanctions On 13 Canadians

https://soundcloud.com/hromadske-radio/russia-slaps-sanctions-on-13

The top two stories dominating Canadian headlines on Monday March 24th were the Malaysia Airlines Flight MH370 and Russia's sanctions against Canada.

Prime Minister Stephen Harper's strong condemnation of Russia's annexation of Crimea has clearly rankled Putin. Canada was the first to impose sanctions against Russia, and is pushing to expel Russia from the G8. Russia responded by slapping travel restrictions against 13 Canadians.

When Liberal MP Irwin Cotler saw his name on the list, he tweeted, "I see my travel ban from Russia as a badge of honor, not a mark of exclusion." The former Justice Minister had once provided legal council to Nelson Mandela, and Soviet-era political prisoner Natan Sharansky.

Until recently, Canada and Russia had enjoyed friendly relations, co-operating on the Arctic Council, holding Canada-Russia Business Summits, expanding trade in areas such as agri-food, agriculture, fuel, energy, construction, housing, and mining.

However, as Putin increasingly curtailed domestic rights and freedoms, public opinion in Canada towards Russia began to shift. A 2013 BBC World Service poll showed that 29% of Canadians viewed Russia positively, while 50% expressed a negative view.

Yesterday I received an angry message from a Russian Canadian who heard me on CTV, commenting that Ukraine appreciated Harper's show of support.

"Do you think Putin really gives two '…' what Harper says or thinks?"

It would seem that Putin does.

28 March 14

Concert for Ukraine: Sold Out

https://soundcloud.com/hromadske-radio/concert-for-ukraine-sold-out

By the time I got to the online box office, all the tickets were sold out. The benefit concert for Ukraine, in the 1,350-seat Mississauga Living Arts Centre, in a suburb of Toronto, was headlined by Maria Burmaka, Brent Carver, Taras Chubai, Serhiy "Foma" Fomenko, whom I've never seen live, the Lemon Bucket Orchestra, and many others. It was organized in co-operation with the Canada Ukraine Foundation, under the artistic direction of Andrey Tarasiuk.

I saw the poster at an art gallery, and made a note to get a ticket. Rushing around with teaching, interviews, lectures, it was the night before that I realized, the concert was happening the next day, on the 28th of March 2014.

Although disappointed that I'll miss out on all the great music, I'm delighted that there will be lots of funds raised, for the victims of the Maidan and the families of the Nebesna Sotnya, the Heavenly Hundred.

And Dr. Ol'ha Bohomolets', the scheduled guest of honor, will get to practice her campaign speech in front of a Canadian audience.

19 April 2014

Separatism and Federalism: A View from Canada

http://hromadskeradio.org/2014/04/19/separatism-and-federalism/
https://soundcloud.com/hromadske-radio/separatism-and-federalism-a

Separatism and federalism are words most Canadians know well. When Quebec held its second referendum on separatism, in 1995, I was in Dnipropetrovsk, Ukraine. Anxiously waiting for the results, I wondered what sort of Canada I would return to, whether there would still be a Canada. The pro-Canadian federalists won by a hair. 50.6% of Quebecers voted 'no' to independence, while 49.4% voted 'yes'.

Canada was set up as a federation in 1867. Through a long process of negotiation, British and French settlers of three colonies reorganized themselves into four Canadian provinces. They decided they'd be better off resisting potential American encroachment by coming together into one state. Over time, other territories joined Canada.

Throughout its history Canada has faced the challenges of balancing federal-provincial relations. It's difficult to accommodate people with diverse regional interests living in the world's second largest geographic country. Particularly problematic has been the relationship between Quebec and the rest of Canada. Quebec was originally colonized by France starting in the 16th century, and even today over 80% of its population is francophone. Although four Prime Ministers have come from Quebec, thirteen have been Anglophone.

In the 1960s a Quiet Revolution began in Quebec. Social change led to political change. Those who felt dominated by the English speaking majority, began advocating separatism. René Lévesque led the movement and created the openly separatist Parti Québécois in 1968. Within a few years, in 1976, he won the Quebec election, and began the push for independence. He passed Bill 101, making French the dominant language in Quebec, and organized a sovereignty referendum in 1980. Then only 40% of the population voted for secession. What followed was a long series of negotiations to reorganize Canada's Constitutional order. In 1982 Quebec's special status was formally recognized.

Interesting to remember, Canada's Prime Minister at the time was Pierre Elliot Trudeau, a Quebecer who wanted Quebec to remain part of Canada.

Tensions between Quebec and the rest of Canada have mostly been in the political realm, apart from a period of violence led by the Marxist-Leninist FLQ in the 1960s. Support for separatism has fluctuated. In the 1990s it was so strong that the Bloc Québécois was the official opposition party in the federal parliament. In 1995 a second Quebec referendum was held. The one I watched from afar.

But in recent years, separatist sentiment has declined dramatically. A few weeks ago, on 7 April, the Parti Québécois lost the provincial election, receiving the lowest popular vote in its history. Federalists, many from Quebec, have been working hard to convince Quebecers to stay in Canada. A concerted policy of economic incentives, granting status of a distinct society, and political infighting among the separatists seem to be convincing most Quebecers.

These days there is much talk of federalism and separatism in Ukraine, and I have been anxiously watching from Canada. Unlike in Canada, though, in Ukraine separatism seems to be stoked from abroad. Legitimate issues are being distorted by a neighbor's pernicious foreign policy agenda, through military intervention. I hope to travel to Ukraine soon, and wonder what kind of Ukraine I will find. Hopefully, one free of foreign troops, and engaged in negotiation on how to re-organize the political system so that all people living in Ukraine feel represented and respected.

23 April 2014

Russia-Canada: Diplomatic Tit-For-Tat

https://soundcloud.com/hromadske-radio/russia-canada-diplomatic-tit

Canadian diplomats rarely get expelled, but on 22 April Margarita Atanasov, first secretary of the immigration section of Canada's Embassy in Moscow, was told to leave Russia. That day Russia's assistant military attaché in Ottawa, Lt.-Col. Yury Bezler, was scheduled to leave Canada. He had been asked to leave on 8 April. The news quickly rose to the top of Canadian headlines.

By coincidence, Russia's Ambassador to Canada, Georgiy Mamedov, was giving a luncheon talk at the Empire Club in Toronto, a conservative discussion forum established in 1903. He made some conciliatory statements, like "We will cut through this suspicion and together we will help Ukrainians come together and live happily and be independent." But when he said that Crimea was always part of Russia, and, "whether you like it or not there is only one legitimate president in Ukraine according to the Ukrainian constitution: Viktor Yanukovych," the usually sedate crowd heckled him. As one audience member shouted, "Not true," and another held up a sign that read, "Lies," the Russian Ambassador said, "Just don't throw pies at me."

Mamedov was critical of Canada, its harsh stance towards Russia over the Ukraine crisis, but tried to downplay the diplomatic expulsion. He said, "Canadians expelled our guy, military attaché, so it's probably we also kicked out some military spy from Moscow. Simple stuff. Nothing relevant in my line of job when I discuss serious security issues." He compared the stand-off with Canada to penalties in playoff hockey.

The National Hockey League Playoffs began last week. Also last week Prime Minister Harper announced that Canada would be sending CF-18 jet fighters to join NATO's operations in Eastern Europe and additional military personnel to Brussels.

The situation in Ukraine and Canada's response is no game.

19 May 2014

Crimean Tatars' Deportation Remembered in Toronto

https://soundcloud.com/hromadske-radio/crimean-tatars-deportation, http://hromadskeradio.org/2014/05/19/crimean-tatars-deportation-remembered-in-toronto-marta-dyczok-reports/

There are only about 200 Crimean Tatars in Toronto. But like Crimean Tatars everywhere, on the 18th of May they gathered to commemorate the date when Stalin deported them from their homeland. This year, which marks the 70th anniversary, the Ukrainian Canadian Congress joined them and offered the Ukrainian National Federation's Trident Hall for the event.

So many people came that the organizers had to keep adding chairs. Politicians from different political parties and levels of government spoke, as did the Consul General of Ukraine and Turkey, various community leaders, children of survivors. Seventy-five-year-old Eldar Muradov, who was filming the event, was introduced as a deportee.

It was a solemn occasion. Many tears could be seen as a clip from the film Haytarma showed a re-enactment of the deportation. But there were children running around, enjoying the Crimean Tatar food that was on offer, giggling, playing. Eight-year-old Arsen Patapov came up when he saw me taking photos and announced, "I can speak Ukrainian!" He had recently arrived in Toronto from Crimea.

As did Elvira Maksudova (Saale), who gave a wonderful rendition of Guzel Qirim to the accompaniment of a violin.

8 June 2014

Ukraine-Canada: A New Phase

https://soundcloud.com/hromadske-radio/hr-en-14-06-08-harper
http://hromadskeradio.org/2014/06/08/ukraine-canada-a-new-phase-marta-dyczok-reports-from-kyiv/

The first foreign leader Petro Poroshenko met with as President, was Canadian Prime Minister Stephen Harper. Harper was the only G7 leader who traveled to Kyiv for the inauguration on June 7th. As Poroshenko was taking his oath, Harper tweeted, "Canada has and will continue to stand with the people of Ukraine."

Canada often gets overshadowed by larger international actors like the EU and the US. But throughout the Euromaidan protests, and after Russia's invasion, Canada had a very active Ukraine policy. Harper consistently made statements condemning violence, calling for peaceful solutions. Canada was one of the first countries to threaten and introduce economic sanctions against corrupt Ukrainian officials, then against Russians after they invaded Ukraine. It also successfully advocated excluding Russia from the G7. Harper visited Kyiv on March 22nd to support the interim government, at a time when things looked bleak.

Ukrainian Canadian Congress President Paul Grod was with Harper then – and again in June. For months, he and the UCC had lobbied the Canadian government to act on Ukraine. They organized support protests throughout Canada, collected and sent money to Maidan activists, and later to the Ukrainian armed forces.

When Poroshenko met the Canadian delegation in Kyiv, he thanked the Canadian government and the Ukrainian diaspora. Noting that Canada was the first Western country that recognized Ukraine's independence in 1991, he said, "We can count on you as our closest friends. I'm convinced that after the inauguration we can begin a new phase of relations between Ukraine and Canada."

16 June 2014

What I Can Do…?

https://soundcloud.com/hromadske-radio/what-i-can-do-marta-dyczok
http://hromadskeradio.org/2014/06/16/what-i-can-do-marta-dyczok-from-kyiv/

I've read a lot about war because I study World War II. Now I find myself in a country that's experiencing war, a new type of 21st century, post-modern, undeclared, creeping war. My friends in Canada, the US, England, and Brazil, keep writing and asking, "How does it feel? What's the mood like?"

Being in the capital Kyiv, where spring is in full bloom and the fighting is hundreds of kilometers away, it feels surreal. Every morning I wake up and turn on the news, like I do back home in Canada. The difference here, is that Donets'k, Luhans'k, Crimea, and Moscow are always the top stories.

All around me are people struggling to cope. They lived through the winter Euromaidan protests, where people were attacked, kidnapped, and killed by their own government because they stood up for themselves. They succeeded in ousting a corrupt President, but are now watching as an enemy, hiding behind masks but carrying heavy weaponry, is taking over their territory and killing.

What's inspiring is seeing people are doing what they can, where they can, and how they can. Journalists are gathering to discuss how to maintain professional standards in conditions of war. Young men are volunteering to go and defend Ukraine's borders, even though the state is not providing them with proper equipment or training. Activists are buying helmets and bullet proof vests online, bringing them across the border, and sending them to the National Guard.

The new president declared a national day of mourning after over 40 people were killed when a plane was shot down. He announced aid would be provided to all the families and called an emergency meeting of the National

Security Council. Priests are praying for the souls of the departed as choirs sing 'Vichnaya pamiat' – which means Eternal Memory. Artists are holding exhibits and concerts to provide society with oases from the constant stress.

What I can do is share this information with you.

23 June 2014

1941-2014: Past Reaching into Present

https://soundcloud.com/hromadske-radio/1941-2014-past-reaching-into
http://hromadskeradio.org/2014/06/23/1941-2014-past-reaching-into-present-professor-of-history-marta-dyczok-from-kyiv/

With war on their territory, perhaps many Ukrainians were not thinking about history on June 22. That day, the anniversary of Germany's attack on the USSR in 1941, their President Petro Poroshenko visited the current war zone. He placed a wreath at a memorial commemorating those killed in the past, and turned his attention to the present. Announcing a unilateral cease fire, he appealed to those shooting to lay down their arms so that peace could be restored. "Both of my grandfathers died during World War II fighting in the Red Army," he told reporters, and expressed fears that a new World War might be brewing.

As most Ukrainians hope for peace, the past continues to cast a heavy shadow over the present. The way history was written and taught in the Soviet era distorted the facts and created a warped historical memory in Ukraine and Russia. Those who did not experience events, or have access to independent sources of information, are struggling to come to terms with what actually happened and understand why. Some continue to believe in old myths constructed by all sides.

For decades, people in the Soviet Union were told that the war started on the 22nd of June in 1941. That day Germany launched Operation Barbarossa and invaded the USSR. What wasn't talked about within the USSR was that the war had actually started in September of 1939 after the Soviet Union and Germany agreed to divide Eastern Europe amongst themselves in the Molotov-Ribbentrop Pact.

This led to the most widespread war in history. It directly involved more than 100 million people from more than 30 countries, and caused between 50 and 85 million fatalities. We may never know the exact figure, but demographers and historians continue to work with statistics and archives. A recent study by Russian historian Vadim Erlikman shows that Ukraine lost over 16% of its population as a result of the war. Of the estimated 6,850,00 killed, 5,200,000 were civilians.

During this conflict a partisan movement sprung up in Western Ukraine that congealed into the Ukrainian Insurgent Army. A significant portion of the fighters came from the Stepan Bandera-led part of the Organization of Ukrainian Nationalists. Their aim was to create an independent Ukraine, but their ideology was right wing and there are some questionable aspects to their activities. They continued to fight for independence into the 1950s and posed a serious threat to the Soviet myth of unity. While demonized in the official Soviet historical narrative, they created their own heroic one.

Today, Russians are being told by their mass media that nationalist-fascists have seized power in Ukraine, that Russians and Russian speakers are being threatened and killed by right wing anti-Semitic banderites, and that the Ukrainian government is killing its own people. These media messages are also being sent into Ukraine. They seem deliberately framed in historical terms to open up old wounds, enflame divisions, and incite hatred.

"The way to stop this war is to stop it in people's heads," Donets'k journalist Serhiy Harmash said recently. As a historian I know nothing is ever black or white. But if people take a clear look at the past and confront the truths and the lies, it may help convince those being spurred to kill that they'd be better off building a future.

1 July 2014

War Echo in Ukrainian Mountains

http://hromadskeradio.org/2014/06/30/war-echo-in-ukrainian-mountains-marta-dyczok-reports-from-carpathians/
https://soundcloud.com/hromadske-radio/war-echo-n-ukrainian-mountains

Teenagers in the Carpathian Mountains are helping Ukraine's war effort. They're collecting funds, buying supplies, and driving them to the other end of their country where the fighting is.

I heard about this during my weekend trip to a picturesque village that I've been visiting for years from a 19-year-old blond woman who just obtained her teaching certificate. She's been volunteering for months, despite her grandmother's and brother's disapproval.

At first she didn't want to talk to me about it, not knowing how I'd react. Opinion in the village is divided. Some, like her, are doing what they can to oppose Russian aggression against Ukraine. Others can't understand why men are fleeing from the east to Western Ukraine, rather than defending themselves against pro-Russian armed separatists and Russians who are invading and killing.

I heard stories about these internally displaced men behaving boorishly. I also heard about locals taking advantage of the situation, falsely using the names of known pro-Ukrainian activist groups for personal gain, and in doing so, discrediting their efforts. My young friend told me about an incident. Some guy wanted a seat in a crowded bus and threatened another passenger who refused to give his up saying, 'I'm from the Right Sector, if you don't give me your seat, we'll come after you."

The Right Sector emerged during Ukraine's winter Euromaidan protests and is controversial because of their right wing ideology and advocating the use of force. But they've been active in opposing Russia's war against Ukraine. "I know that guy's not part of the Right Sector," said the young woman.

Her disapproving grandmother, who was listening to our conversation, joined in. "It was like that during World War II," she said. "All sorts of horrible thing were done by people, claiming to be part of the Ukrainian Insurgent Army, to discredit them."

I remember hearing stories from the elderly woman's brother about what had gone on in that village during the Second World War. He'd showed me the basement where he and his high school buddies hid Ukrainian partisans who were fighting against the Red Army.

There's no fighting in the Carpathian Mountains today, and his great-niece is not sheltering partisans. She's applying to university in the fall, and going abroad for the summer. But she inherited her great-uncle's spirit, and is now helping to send supplies to men who are not running away from – but going into – the zone of combat and resisting an invading aggressor.

8 July 2014

Dreamland in Kyiv

https://soundcloud.com/hromadske-radio/dreamland-in-kyiv-marta-dyczok
http://hromadskeradio.org/2014/07/08/dreamland-in-kyiv-marta-dyczok-reports-from-a-festival-in-ukraine-s-capital/

Ukraine's famous musical artistic innovator Oleh Skrypka delivered a much needed oasis of beauty over the weekend in Kyiv, hosting his 11th annual Kraina Mriy festival. It means Dreamland.

On the festival's web page, www.krainamriy.com/ he posted this message:

"Dear Dreamers! More and more often we are hearing that what's happening in Ukraine, and the entire world, is not just an intensification of old social and political problems, not simply the aggression of one state against another. What we are seeing right now is the collapse of an old world order and movement away from a no longer viable model of society. To get through these turbulent times we need to find a new model, to propose new ideas, to create an ideology that can inspire many. So I invite everybody, right now, to creative and social cooperation."

Tons of people showed up, even though the festival was moved to the Feofania Park on the outskirts of the city, and not easy to get to. Driving there with friends, the city center was clear of traffic, but the road leading into the park was jam packed with cars, mini-buses, and pedestrians.

Musicians, artisans, writers, chefs, story-tellers, and vendors from all over Ukraine and beyond, filled the well-tended, picturesque, sprawling park. There was a literary Dreamland, an ethno-fashion zone, a children's area full of hands-on activities like making traditional toys from straw, a Cossack entertainment zone, a Crimean Tatar stage, master classes of seemingly everything, local beer and kefir tastings, a zone of free creativity, and much more.

Strolling down the main alley I saw Soviet-era dissident turned politician turned diplomat turned writer Lev Lukianenko. Humbly standing in an embroidered shirt, he was selling his books. These days, almost everyone is wearing an embroidered shirt. He wore his decades ago, well before it was trendy.

Sounds of drums attracted my attention. I followed the sounds down the hill and discovered the ethno-drumming sun rhythms circle. Under a tent people were sitting on the grass, on cushions, stools, and turned towards a few musicians playing the traditional hutsul drymba, mini-trembita, and bells. African drums lay all around for anyone to pick up and join in. So I did.

Looking to rejoin my friends I came across a burly blacksmith showing off his skills, a little girl posing on a straw horse, heard a man telling traditional tales, saw a woman painting a ceramic bird, watched people dancing to the sounds from the Folklore stage.

When I found my friends we sat down for a bite to eat, I saw Skrypka casually walking past. I jumped up to thank him for the festival, and noticed that he was carrying a small plastic bag. "What's in the bag?" I asked. He reached in, pulled something out and handed it to me, "It's a turnip," he said. "Enjoy!" It was delicious.

On the eve of World War II, Winston Churchill had said, "The arts are essential to any complete national life." As Ukrainians fight to withstand the undeclared war that is being waged against them by Russia, artists like Oleh Skrypka are fighting with positivity. While some are calling for a boycott of Russian goods and artists, he's suggesting a different approach. "Let's buy Ukrainian products, listen to Ukrainian music. Let's protect ourselves, support one another, fight to protect our rights, our country. We need to know who we are and build our country anew, in an active and constructive way.

14 July 2014

Her Name Means Hope: A Pensioner Helps Ukrainian Armed Forces

https://soundcloud.com/hromadske-radio/her-name-means-hope-a
http://hromadskeradio.org/2014/07/14/her-name-means-hope-a-pensioner-helps-ukrainian-armed-forces-marta-dyczok-reports-from-kyiv/

84-year-old Nadiya regularly makes phone donations to Ukraine's National Guard. She now lives in a village about an hour away from Kyiv, and finds it hard to get around without her cane. But she stays on top of the news. "You know that over a hundred of our men have been killed," she said, as I sat in her living room, and watched her eyes fill with tears.

Born in the same village as Taras Shevchenko, she's a distant relative of Ukraine's national bard. During Stalin's terror, her father was imprisoned because he refused to join the collective farm. The family survived the Holodomor artificial famine because a kind official helped her illiterate mother write an appeal that allowed them to keep one cow.

Nadiya went on to become a school teacher. Her brother, Seriozha, went to Kyiv to study in a Military Academy. War broke out and he was sent to the front. He was a tank commander and died near Smolensk. She remembers the date precisely, 19 December 1942, even though she had to look up the phone number to her one remaining sister who she calls all the time.

Nadiya told me, "Our village deputy, Larysa, was kind enough to come by and take my donation for the village collection to buy food supplies for the men fighting today." She added apologetically, "You understand, it's hard for me to get down to the shop."

She'd heard stories of a neighbor, who'd spent her working life in Russia and came back to Ukraine to retire, refusing to donate. "Imagine," Nadiya said. "She never contributed to Ukraine's economy but draws her pension from the Ukrainian state. Now, when the country is at war, she says, it's the state's responsibility to fund the army."

I didn't dare ask what Nadiya's pension is, but know that her daughters support her financially.

As I was leaving the village, Nadiya insisted that I take some cucumbers I'd helped pick from her garden and some apricots and cherries from her orchard. She seemed very disappointed that I wouldn't take more as she smiled, wished me health, happiness, and peace.

19 July 2014

International Headlines on Malaysian Airline Tragedy as Seen from Kyiv

https://soundcloud.com/hromadske-radio/international-headlines-on
http://hromadskeradio.org/2014/07/19/international-headlines-on-malaysian-airliner-tragedy-as-seen-from-kyiv-marta-dyczok-reports/

News of the Malaysia Airlines tragedy immediately hit the international headlines. CBC called me for an interview as the story was just breaking. They then went with an aviation expert which I think was a good decision. They chose to focus on the question how the civilian airline was shot down near Grabovo on July 17th.

Watching the story unfold, I noticed that the first international reports were tentative. Canada's national CTV ran the headline, "MH17 reportedly shot down over Ukraine." They cited Ukrainian government spokespeople as the source. An hour later the headline had changed, to "Malaysia airliner shot down over Ukraine."

The New York Times also quoted Ukrainian officials in their first story called "Jetliner Explodes Over Ukraine; Struck by Missile, Officials Say."

Information was widely reported but with qualifiers. Everyone circulated the audio recordings Ukraine's Secret Service made public. But most shared the BBC's tone, which commented, "Ukrainian authorities have released what they say are intercepted phone conversations, between pro-Russian separatists and what appear to be Russian military officers, saying that separatists shot down Malaysia Airlines flight MH17."

The same caution is used with information from the other side. For example, the Toronto Star wrote, "Ukraine rebels claim to have found flight MH17's recorders."

The key question running through all the reporting is about Russia's involvement. Everyone's condemning the act, demanding a full investigation, and expressing condolences to families of the dead.

One Canadian was on that flight. All Canadian media reported on this. A CBC TV producer coming to Ukraine contacted me as she was heading for the airport. She was looking how to help the family.

I saw only one international report about the 20 Ukrainian civilians killed in Luhans'k the following day by the so-called separatists.

27 July 2014

An Unexpected Encounter in Kyiv

https://soundcloud.com/hromadske-radio/a-rarest-kind-of-handshake
http://hromadskeradio.
org/2014/07/27/a-rarest-kind-of-handshake-marta-dyczok-s-unexpected-
encounter-in-kyiv/

I saw Ukraine's Prime Minister on my way home Friday evening. Arseniy Yatseniuk was walking down Hrushevs'ka Street, from Parliament, towards the Cabinet of Ministers building.

I spotted him because he's a little taller than the men he was walking with. "Look, it's Yatseniuk," I said to my friends, pulled out my camera, and started snapping away. He noticed, so I walked up, held out my hand, and introduced myself. "Where are you from?" he asked. "Canada," I answered.

Given the week he'd had, I was amazed how calm he looked, and how he was so casually friendly. Just the other day, the usually restrained lawyer-economist turned politician gave an emotional speech to Parliament. He submitted his resignation, saying that he could not continue, when elected MPs refused to adopt laws that would release additional funds for the war effort, and the ruling coalition dissolved.

In my opinion, he's been doing a tremendous job since taking over the government after corrupt president Yanukovych fled five months ago. So, I told him so and added that I'd said the same on Canadian national television when news of his resignation broke. He smiled, modestly, and said "thanks."

My friends wanted to get a picture with the PM, and he seemed chuffed. As we were gathering around for the shot, he graciously said, "May I introduce you to my colleague, Oleksander Turchynov, the Parliamentary Speaker. Perhaps you'd like him to be in the photo as well?" Of course we agreed.

Photograph by William Risch

Other passers-by also stopped to shake Yatseniuk's hand and thank him for the work he was doing. He took the time to speak to each of them before getting into the car that was waiting for him. Later I learned that he was on his way to appear on a live political talk show where he appealed for national unity.

28 July 2014

Recovering from Frontline Wounds in Kyiv

https://soundcloud.com/hromadske-radio/recovering-from-frontline
http://hromadskeradio.org/2014/07/28/recovering-from-frontline-wounds-in-kyiv-marta-dyczok-shares-her-visit-to-a-military-hospital/

The military hospital was founded in Kyiv in 1755. Today it houses soldiers wounded in what's called the Anti-Terrorist Operation in eastern Ukraine's Donbas region.

I'd walked past its tree lined walls on my way home from the archives in previous summers, not really paying much attention to it.

Now soldiers with machine guns guard the entrance. But they looked pretty relaxed on the sunny afternoon when I arrived with friend and a basket of fruit. We asked how to get to the wounded, and offered them some. "Thank you, but we're not allowed," they said, eyeing the basket. They directed us to the volunteer headquarters, and we walked in.

Seeing a map, I took out my camera and photographed it. One of the guards rushed up and said, "No photographs, please, this is a military installation, it's not allowed." I apologized. "You'll have to erase the photo you took," he said apologetically. "You understand, if it was my superior, he'd confiscate your camera."

Inside the walls I saw an elegant, park like environment, with neatly tended gardens and old buildings in a courtyard formation. People strolling around casually. We couldn't remember which archway to look for so stopped a passing car and asked, offering the uniformed soldier fruit. He took a plumb, and a pear, and when he was reaching for more I stopped him and said, "they're for the wounded." My friend interrupted me and encouraged him to take as much as he wanted. "He's been to the war zone and has been beaten," she explained to me as we walked on. She'd seen it in his eyes.

The volunteer station was full of people. Hallways lined with bags of fruit, dried goods, medicine, clothes, all neatly organized. The volunteers liked our basket so instead of asking us to just leave it in the hall, they agreed to escort us while we distributed the fruit.

Walking through the grounds we saw all sorts of wounded. Our escort described them to us. "That young man is 30," she said. A few people were helping him walk "He used to be a kick boxer," our guide continued: "When the fighting started he volunteered for one of the battalions, raised money for his own equipment and went to the war zone. He didn't have enough for a helmet, but went anyway. He sustained a head injury and is now missing part of his brain plate."

As we offered him our basket, his kind eyes just looked straight ahead. "He can't see, or hear," said the woman holding his elbow. It was his mother. "Why don't you select what he likes?" my friend suggested. The mother took a few grapes, some pears. "How about an apple?" I suggested. "No, he doesn't like apples," the mother answered. So I took some more grapes and placed them in the palm of his hand, watching as his fingers curled around the sun warmed fruit. His eyes were open but had a look of not understanding what was happening. Something many Ukrainians must be feeling.

There were two men sitting in a gazebo. One asked if he could take some fruit for his girlfriend. The other would only take one plum. I encouraged him to take more, but he politely refused and said, "there are many others here."

We were then taken into one of the buildings, a recovery ward. The high ceilinged hallway was silent, except for the sounds of our footsteps.

In room 11 we met two parachutists. Each was missing an arm. One was able to sit up and select his fruit. The other couldn't move, so his mother took some for him, as he smiled and profusely thanked us.

I didn't want to intrude on any more pain, but wasn't ready to leave. Seeing a group of men chatting on a bench, I suggested that we sit on the one next to them.

A woman with long, flowing, dark hair was pushing a young man in a wheelchair on the path next to us. My friend recognized her and said, "That woman is very wealthy. She comes here every day and talks to the wounded men. The one in the wheelchair is 19 years old, the same age as her son, and has lost a leg. She's paying for an artificial one."

7 August 2014

Far Away, Yet So Close: Leaving Kyiv for Toronto

http://hromadskeradio.org/2014/08/07/far-far-away-yet-so-close-marta-dyczok-reports-on-leaving-kyiv-for-toronto/
https://soundcloud.com/hromadske-radio/far-far-away-yet-so-close

A young woman with long blond hair drove me to Kyiv airport. She dreams about traveling. "Where would you like to go?" I asked. "To an island," she answered. "The further away from here, the better."

She lives in a country at war, even though war has not been declared. Every morning the news headlines start with casualty figures, reports how many times Russia fired into Ukrainian territory, what was destroyed.

My young driver admitted that she doesn't watch the news, because it makes her cry.

There was extra security at Boryspil airport. New metal detectors have been installed at every entrance. But the security staff were courteous and friendly, as were the border guards. But they now wear fatigues. The woman who checked my passport was efficient, taking longer with some passengers than others. After carefully examining my travel document she smiled. And wished me a safe flight.

The aroma of war had floated onto the airplane flying out of Kyiv. It wasn't until I'd landed in Frankfurt airport for my stop-over, that it felt like I had left the war zone.

I hadn't wanted to leave, but needed to go home and prepare for the fall term.

In Toronto a tall, dark-skinned man was my cab driver. I apologized that my suitcase was heavy, but he lifted into the trunk with little effort. Opening the door for me he said, "You look tired, where have you come from?" "Ukraine." I answered. "You know there's a war going on there."

"Yes," he said. "Terrible. All those innocent people being killed."

As he drove me through the peaceful streets of Toronto, I remembered saying goodbye to Ukraine's National Security Council spokesperson, col. Andriy Lysenko. He's the one who prepares and reads the twice daily updates on the war that my Kyiv cab driver can't listen to. "You're leaving? Why?" he asked. I explained that I had to go back to my university. "Come back soon," he said. "We're going to win and invite you to the victory ceremony."

I can't wait to get on the plane for that.

8 August 2014

Ottawa Takes Lead in Imposing Sanctions

http://hromadskeradio.org/2014/08/08/ottawa-takes-lead-in-imposing-sanctions-a-view-from-canada/
https://soundcloud.com/hromadske-radio/ottawa-takes-lead-in-imposing

Ukraine is once again the top story in Canadian media.

"We will not be intimidated," Canada's Industry Minister James Moore said on the 7th of August. He added that the world needs to continue to stand firm against Russia, despite the escalation of sanctions.

Canada took the lead in imposing sanctions against the corrupt Yanukovych regime and then against Russia. Now it appears to be taking the lead in another sphere.

The day that NATO Secretary General, Anders Fogh Rasmussen, arrived in Kyiv and told Ukraine's President Poroshenko that, "NATO's support for the sovereignty and territorial integrity of Ukraine is unwavering," Canada loaded up a CC-130J Hercules military plane with non-lethal military equipment and sent it to Ukraine. Prime Minister Stephen Harper announced that this was just the first in a series of flights that would deliver up to 5 million dollars' worth of helmets, ballistic eyewear, protective vests, first-aid kits, tents, and sleeping bags, to help Ukrainians secure their eastern border against Russian aggression.

The flights are leaving from Canadian Forces Base Trenton, in Ontario.

16 August 2014

What They Want and Don't Want to Know About Ukraine in Ontario

https://soundcloud.com/hromadske-radio/what-they-want-and-dont-want
http://hromadskeradio.org/2014/08/16/what-they-want-and-don-t-want-to-know-about-ukraine-in-ontario-marta-dyczok-on-her-first-day-at-uwo/

"Thank goodness you're back safe!" Bibi said as she jumped up to hug me. "I was so worried about you." Bibi is the administrator of the Political Science Department at my university. She'd been posting my reports from Ukraine on the departmental website throughout the summer. "Tell me what it was like, what's going on now?" she wanted to know. I told her that I had not been in danger, that Kyiv is far from the war zone.

Teresa, the Graduate Secretary, came over. "What's Putin doing?" she asked. I tried to explain and passed around some chocolates I'd brought for them. "They're made by Ukraine's President," I said smiling. Teresa looked puzzled, but Bibi said, "Yes, I remember, you wrote about that in the Toronto Star when Poroshenko was elected president that he made his fortune in chocolate." They asked about the images on the chocolates. Bibi chose one that had a photo from Crimea. Teresa picked one with storks, and said it would be OK if I submitted marks for student essays that had come in while I was away a bit late.

Life at Western University continues much as before. I sat through a Workload Committee meeting. We discussed how much each professor should be teaching. While trying to focus on preparing a document that would be fair to everyone, part of my mind was on the 280 trucks headed from Russia to Ukraine. I was asked to speak about that on CTV, and apologized that I had to leave the meeting early. Rob walked out with me and wanted to hear all about Ukraine.

Dusan, the CTV technician, met me at the entrance. He rushed me into the studio and began wiring me up for sound. I was a bit late because traffic was terrible. A glass of water was waiting for me. He'd remembered that I get thirsty in air conditioned spaces. Afterwards, as he escorted me out, he said, "It's terrible. What's going to happen?" Last time I was there he'd told me he's originally from the former Yugoslavia. He understands war.

Not everybody here is interested in what's going on in Ukraine. Some colleagues I see in the hall say, "Hi, how are things?" and walk by not waiting to hear the answer. Friends I met up with one evening wanted to tell me about their vacations, rather than hear about people being killed in some far away country.

I remember the day when I'd watched volunteers take a military oath to defend Ukraine in Nova Petrivka, and then others near the Bohdan Khmel'nyts'kyi statue in central Kyiv. Afterwards I walked down the hill towards the Maidan, and popped into the underground shopping mall Globus to escape the heat. There, other young men were casually sipping lattes and checking their mobile devices.

But I also remember the what journalist I'd been with at the oath taking ceremony said, "We're going to win this war, because those guys you just saw have spirit."

Hoping that each of them comes back to a welcome like the one I got from Bibi.

15 September 2014

Impressions on the Maidan Exhibit in Toronto

https://soundcloud.com/hromadske-radio/maidan-exhibition-in-toronto
http://hromadskeradio.org/2014/09/15/maidan-exhibition-in-toronto-marta-dyczok-shares-impressions/

The largest Ukrainian festival in North America happens in my neighborhood. In Bloor West Village in Toronto. This year it was held on the weekend of the 12th to 14th of September.

Canadian-Ukrainian journalist Yury Klufas began the tradition 18 years ago. He wanted to celebrate the fact that so many Ukrainians live in Toronto, to share the heritage. And it just grew. There's a parade, musicians, artisans, vendors, food, book stalls. A few streets get closed off to traffic, public transit is re-routed to allow pedestrians to enjoy. Politicians from all levels of government come to the official parts, looking for Ukrainian votes.

This year there was a special Maidan exhibit. It was organized by the people who have been following political events in Ukraine and organizing support actions since last November. Among other things, they reconstructed a version of the 'yolka' that I'd seen on it's last legs in Kyiv in the summer, and has since been moved. 'Oh, that's where it's gone,' wrote my poet friend Volodymyr from Kyiv when I posted a photo of the TO 'yolka' on Facebook.

I was a bit worried that the unexpected cold snap and rain predictions might mean that fewer people would show up to the festival this year. And with war continuing in eastern Ukraine, perhaps some would not be in a festive mood.

But the streets were packed. As before, people came from near and far. The first person I bumped into was my friend Dennis. He's driven a few hundred kilometers from Ottawa, as he does every year for the festival.

There was an Open University this year too, organized by Euromaidan Toronto. They also put out a piano, photos, films, and tires.

Musicians from Ukraine are always invited to perform at the festival. On Friday night the Mukachevo band Rock-H was the musical headliner. I caught part of their performance with my friend Ira who's originally from Chortkiv.

The food was great, and diverse. The first day I opted for gourmet varenyky, slightly overpriced but delicious. On the second day, rushing from my lecture at the Open University to meet my favorite nephew, who'd come in from St. Catherine's, I chose lobster poutine from our local fish and chips place. They were doing a festival promotion.

On the way I'd been stopped by journalist Andriy Holovatyi. "I'd like to ask you about Hromadske Radio, among other things," he said. "They're doing really interesting things and I'd like to hear more."

So I chatted with him in a sound booth on the street that was being live streamed. Around us sounds of music floated past. Some people were talking politics while others enjoying drinks – as people do at festivals.

19 September 2014

Ukraine President's Visit as Seen by North American Media

http://hromadskeradio.org/2014/09/19/ukraine-president-s-visit-as-seen-by-north-american-media-by-marta-dyczok/
https://soundcloud.com/hromadske-radio/ukraine-presidents-visit-as

For once, Ukraine was in the headlines with a good news story. President Poroshenko's visits to Ottawa and Washington this week were leading stories in Canadian and American media over the past few days. Along with the Scottish referendum, the growing Ebola crisis, the ISIS terrorist threat, and controversial Toronto mayor Rob Ford being diagnosed with cancer.

Canada's two leading national TV networks, CBC and CTV, live streamed Poroshenko's speech to the joint session of Parliament and Senate on the Hill on Wednesday 18 September – a rare occurrence. Minutes after the speech, the wires were reporting the key moments, the numerous standing ovations.

"Canada is a friend indeed" was one of the Poroshenko's most popular quotes that a number of media outlets used as a headline.

The following day, American TV channels also showed the standing ovations Poroshenko received from the joint session of US Congress and Senate. They showed clips of the speech that Ukraine's president delivered with panache, in impeccable English, using terminology that Americans are used to – like "It is the war for the free world," and "Aggression against one democratic nation is aggression against all of us."

After meeting with US President Obama, Poroshenko appeared on CNN with Wolf Blitzer. When the award winning journalist asked him point blank whether the US had agreed to Ukraine's request for major non-NATO ally status – that countries like Japan, South Korea, and Israel enjoy – Poroshenko answered frankly: "My answer would be, again, very straightforward. The answer of President Obama was no," and then he went on to explain the reasoning.

A story on the radio caught my attention in the evening as I was driving home. It was further down the headlines about a deal signed between Canada and the US on energy cooperation. Both are looking to diversity their global markets. US Energy Secretary, Ernest Moniz, and Canadian Natural Resources Minister Greg Rickford both spoke of collective energy security. What caught my attention was that they both said they're looking at Ukraine, want to help 'Ukraine's transition to a more independent energy strategy,' and to help lessen its energy dependency on Russia. But, this is a long term plan.

22 September 2014

The New Face of Canadian Diplomacy in Ukraine

http://hromadskeradio.org/2014/09/22/new-face-of-canadian-diplomacy-in-ukraine-by-marta-dyczok/
https://soundcloud.com/hromadske-radio/new-face-of-canadian-diplomacy

Canada has appointed a new ambassador to Ukraine. Toronto born Roman Waschuk will become Canada's ninth diplomatic representative in Kyiv this autumn. He'll be coming from Belgrade, where he's served as Canada's ambassador since 2011, with concurrent accreditation to Macedonia and Montenegro. He speaks English, French, German, Russian, Ukrainian, Polish, and Serbian/Montenegrin.

Mr. Waschuk is no stranger to Ukraine, or the post-Soviet space. After completing his MA in History at the University of Toronto in 1985, he joined the Canadian Foreign Service. His first diplomatic posting with Foreign Affairs, was in the Moscow Embassy in 1988, where he served as political secretary through 1991. We'd grown up together in Toronto and met up again in Moscow in 1991. I'd decided to pursue a PhD, and had gone to Moscow to do archival research. When I couldn't find housing right away, he and his wife kindly let me use their guest room for a while.

A few years later, in 1994, Mr. Waschuk was appointed Political Counsellor in Canada's Embassy in Ukraine, where he served until 1998. So we saw each other again since I was living in Kyiv at the time. During those years, Ukraine signed the Budapest Memorandum and adopted a constitution.

After Kyiv there was the usual rotation to Ottawa, where Mr. Waschuk served as Deputy Director of the European Union Division, and the Policy Planning Division. He was then posted to Canada's Berlin Embassy (2002-2007), as Political Counsellor, then Minister-Counsellor. Back in Ottawa after that, there were positions in the Global Partnership, Biological Non-Proliferation, Stabilization and Reconstruction Programs. And then the Ambassadorship in

Serbia.

We last saw each other in Toronto in late August. I was watching the tail end of the live political talk show Svoboda Slova with Andriy Kulykov, when Roman and his wife stopped by. So, they joined me in watching. The then still Ambassador to Serbia recognized the participants in the Ukrainian show. "Didn't that man work for Tymoshenko?" he asked about one of the experts. "As far as I know, he still does," I answered.

Canada's Foreign Affairs Minister John Baird, made the announcement about new diplomatic appointments last Friday 19 September, a few days after Ukraine's President Poroshenko had visited Ottawa. With everything else going on, I didn't see it until the weekend. The same press release said that Martine Moreau became Canada's new ambassador to Kuwait, and Troy Lulashnyk – who had served in Kyiv – was being sent to be Canada's ambassador in the Arab Republic of Egypt.

14 October 2014

Movies Move Canadians to Helps Ukrainians

http://hromadskeradio.org/2014/10/14/movies-move-canadians-to-help-ukrainians-marta-dyczok-reports-from-mississauga/
https://soundcloud.com/hromadske-radio/movies-move-canadians-to-help

The Toronto Ukrainian Film Festival screened three movies this week. It was a benefit to raise funds for imprisoned Ukrainian film maker Oleh Sentsov. One was Senstov's 2011 film Gamer (Гамер). The second was Oles Sanin's Поводир (The Guide). I made it to the third, a Sunday matinee. It was Anatoliy Mateshko's *The Trumpeter* (Трубач), playing at the CineStarz cinema in Mississauga.

A group of activists and organizations have been screening films from Ukraine in Toronto since the Euromaidan protests began last fall. They're usually shown in small, independent cinemas, and have included a number of the Babylon 13 films. This week's screening was sponsored by the Ukrainian Credit Union, Kontakt TV and UkrStream TV, and the Ukrainian Culture Festival.

"Enjoy the newest movies from Ukraine and help in the fight to defend human rights!" was on the latest poster that caught my attention. It also said that "all the money raised during the events will go to help Oleg Sentsov." So, I went.

The first person I saw in the crowd was Nastya, a friend from choir, with her two kids. As I looked around the movie theatre, I realized that most people had come with their kids. "I think this is the children's feature" I said apologetically to my mother, as we settled into our seats. "That's OK" she said smiling, "you're my child."

I had really hoped to see a film by Sentsov. But The Trumpeter had a nice message about following your dreams, overcoming life's challenges. And, it had a happy ending. As I hope will the case in the real life story of Sentsov.

4 November 2014

Passage Is Forbidden: But Who Will Stop You?

http://hromadskeradio.org/2014/11/04/passage-is-forbidden-but-who-will-stop-you-marta-dyczok-reports-from-ukrainian-russian-border/
https://soundcloud.com/hromadske-radio/passage-is-forbidden-but-who

I was at the Ukrainian-Russian border recently. Just outside the Volfine village in the Sumy oblast. It was a field. For a while I couldn't figure out where the border was.

Our driver didn't really want to take us there, because the road was well off the main highway and full of potholes. He didn't want to damage his car.

He kept saying, 'the border is just over there," and pointing out the window.

"Where?" we asked. But he just kept repeating the same phrase and pointing across the field.

Eventually we asked him to stop and decided to walk.

"Do you have good walking shoes?" Antoine asked.

"Yes, of course, let's go!" I answered. And we set off.

Antoine and I were Canadian election observers. We had arrived in Ukraine to monitor the October early parliamentary election, and deployed to the Sumy oblast. As luck would have it, the areas we were assigned to cover borders with Russia.

A number of polling stations are located in villages along the border. So we went to visit them to see how election preparations were going. While in Pavlivka, we asked the head of the village election commission how close we were to the border with Russia.

"About 3 kilometers" answered the smiling, heavy-set, woman. "The next village over is partly in Russia", she added. When we asked to explain, she said that the way the borders were drawn, parts of people's gardens had ended up in the Russian Federation. So they had special documents to do their gardening, to be able to walk across their gardens.

"Can we go?" I asked eagerly.

"Oh no, you would need a visa," she replied calmly.

Intrigued, we decided to investigate. To see what the Ukrainian-Russian border looked like in rural Sumy. After all, heavy military equipment had been transferred into Ukraine from Russia for months in two border oblasts further south, in Donets'k and Luhans'k, where there's a war going on.

It was a sunny but cold day. As we were driving, I was struck by the beauty of the countryside and that it was so deserted. No people, buildings, traffic. Just fields, trees, sky. The winter wheat had been planted in neat rows in the black earth.

But, no signs of a border.

As we walked down a path between the fields, Antoine and I wondered how we would know where the border was. We even joked about sirens sounding as we tripped an invisible wire. But instead a dog began barking and running towards us from a farmhouse in the distance. We stopped. Eventually a woman came out. I waved and called out to her, but she didn't respond. But she did call off the dog. So we kept approaching the farm. A young man appeared, so I called out to him, introduced myself, and asked where the border was.

Like our driver, he said, "it's just over there."

"Where?" we asked, feeling like tourists. Because all we could see was a field and some trees.

"Over there," he pointed.

"How far, and how will we know when we get there?" we insisted in knowing.

"About 20 meters, you'll see a black line on the ground," he said, as if it was a silly question. But I thanked him and extended my hand once again. This time he took and shook it. Something he had not done when I'd introduced myself.

So we kept walking. It was freezing cold but I knew we were close.

Antoine noticed a black line on the ground, which to me looked like just another path, like other ones we'd passed. Could this be the border? I scanned the horizon and spotted a sign. It was too far away to make out what it said, and the zoom on Antoine's camera did not help.

"Let's go see what it says," he suggested. For the first time in our adventure I hesitated. Suddenly I had visions of spikes appearing from beneath the ground, sirens going off, helicopters arriving. "You go first," I said. So he did. Nothing happened, so I followed.

We reached the sign. It was blue and white. "Attention. State Border of Ukraine. Do not cross," it said.

So we took photos, on the Ukrainian side, of course, or at least as well as we could tell.

Then we started walking back.

Antoine had noticed a car parked along the path we'd walked along. Looking to the right, I spotted two men, in camouflage, carrying machine guns, walking in the opposite direction. "Take a photo and let's go," I said. So we got their backs. They didn't see us.

Then the phone rang. "Are you guys OK?" our translator wanted to know. "We're fine, but freezing," Antoine assured her.

When we finally got back to the car, they were visibly relieved. They had seen a car with two armed men in uniform appear shortly after we went to look for the border.

Antoine and I were just happy to be back in a warm car. And shocked at how casual the border between two countries in a state of undeclared war can be.

11 November 2014

A Red Poppy, Also for the War in Ukraine

http://hromadskeradio.
org/2014/11/11/a-red-poppy-also-for-the-war-in-ukraine-by-marta-dyczok/
https://soundcloud.com/hromadske-radio/a-red-poppy-also-for-the-war

On 11 November Canadians mark Remembrance Day. We wear poppies and at 11:00 AM we pause to remember all those who lay down their lives in wars to protect our freedoms. The tradition began in England at the end of World War I, in what writer H.G. Wells called "the war to end all war".

The 11th hour, on the 11th day, of the 11th month was chosen for the commemoration. That's when the armistice came into effect, ending one of the deadliest conflicts in human history. Over 16 million dead, 20 million wounded.

The poppy was chosen as the symbol for blood spilled in war, and also new growth amidst the devastation of war. It was inspired by a poem. *In Flanders Fields.* Canadian physician Lt. Col. John McCrae wrote it after burying a friend and fellow soldier in 1915. Most Canadians know at least a few rows by heart:

In Flanders fields the poppies blow
Between the crosses, row on row,
That mark our place; and in the sky
The larks, still bravely singing, fly
Scarce heard amid the guns below.

A year ago I commemorated Remembrance Day with a friend who was visiting from Ukraine. It just so happened that we met on 11 November for a morning coffee. At 11:00, I asked him to join me in a moment of silence.

At the time, I couldn't have imagined that Ukraine would once again be experiencing war, albeit an undeclared one. That I'd be listening to daily reports by Ukrainian Col. Andriy Lysenko on how many killed, wounded, what infrastructure was destroyed.

Or that I'd hear a new inspiring poem about war. It was read in a raspy voice on Hromadske Radio by volunteer fighter Borys Humeniuk on 23 September. He himself said the title, "The Testament," (Zapovit) following national bard Taras Shevchenko, was immodest. But it was full of hope.

This 11 November I'll be remembering not only those long dead from war, but also those killed in the past few months, in my living memory. And looking forward to the day when war is over. And, as soon as I get a copy of the text, trying to memorize a new poem.

I've already got my poppy.

18 November 2014

A Sweater to Save a Life

http://hromadskeradio.
org/2014/11/18/a-sweater-to-save-a-life-by-marta-dyczok-to-be-continued/
https://soundcloud.com/hromadske-radio/a-sweater-to-save-a-life-by

"I have a nice warm sweater that I'm going to bring in next week", my 80 something year old friend said. We were having coffee after church, as we often do. We had just learned that our church is collecting warm clothes, socks, sleeping bags, and funds for Ukrainians fighting against the Russian led war.

The campaign is called 'Save a Life.' It's part of a joint initiative by the Ukrainian Canadian Congress, the Ukrainian Catholic Eparchy of Toronto and Eastern Canada, and the Department of the Patriarchal Curia, of the Ukrainian Greek Catholic Church for Pastoral Care in the Armed Forces of Ukraine.

"Please be generous," the church bulletin reads. The Ukrainian Catholic Women's League has organized collection boxes in the church hall.

In the novel I'm reading there's a scene where women are knitting socks and gathering warm things to send to the men fighting overseas during World War I. Who could have thought that a hundred years later women would need to be doing this again?

Hopefully my friend's sweater will reach a guy like Nick. I came across his Facebook post where he wrote,

"Hallo my dear friends. My name is Nick. I am ordinary Ukrainian soldier. I participate war at the Eastern Ukraine. Last battle I participated was the battle at Donets'k Airport. That is why I am being called 'Cyborg'. Separatists call us

Cyborgs because we managed to stand defending airport buildings 24/7. They were amassed the way we take the battle. Ordinary soldiers 200 approximately against thousands of Russian soldiers which Mr. Putin claim that they get lost and somehow appeared near Donets'k Airport buildings in Ukraine 300 kilometers from Russian border with guns and armor well equipped etc. & suddenly started to shoot at Ukrainians without any reason. Well we started to shoot back. I am ready to write more and answer the questions u ask. Sorry for mistakes. To be continued."

25 November 2014

Words and Reality: Reflections on Hromadske Radio's Broadcast

http://hromadskeradio.org/2014/11/25/words-and-reality-reflections-on-hromadske-radio-s-broadcast-by-dr-marta-dyczok/
https://soundcloud.com/hromadske-radio/words-and-reality-reflections

Canada officially recognized the Holodomor as a genocide back in 2008. This year, on the official commemoration day, Prime Minister Stephen Harper issued a statement in which he said, "On this somber day, let us join with Ukrainians in Canada and around the world in remembering the victims of this genocide." He also said, "We continue to stand with the people of Ukraine in the face of the Putin regime's illegal occupation of the Crimean Peninsula and its military aggression in Eastern Ukraine."[6]

Earlier that day I had listened to the official spokesman of Ukraine's National Security and Defense Council give his daily update on the situation in the Donbas. "Terrorist fighters are intensifying shelling against the positions of the Ukrainian forces in the ATO," col. Lysenko told reporters, and provided details. Officially Ukraine continues to describe the war in Donets'k and Luhans'k as an Anti-Terrorist Operation, while they document the numbers of Russian military convoys crossing into Ukraine.

On Sunday, while listening to Hromadske Radio's live broadcast, I heard a caller talking about "the junta". When journalist Andriy Kulykov asked her

---

[6] See more at: http://pm.gc.ca/eng/news/2014/11/22/statement-prime-minister-canada-81st-anniversary-holodomor#sthash.5ew0lk2w.dpuf

what she was referring to, she answered, "the Maidan". This was a few days after many in Kyiv, and the world, commemorated the beginning of the Ukrainian protests that took on that name and toppled a corrupt president. And, the new president officially named those killed during the protests as national heroes. The official narrative from Moscow continues to refer to the Maidan protests as a coup, a junta. The infamous Russia Today recently ran an op-ed on the "Euromaidan 1st birthday: How the Kiev coup grew".

Words coming from official sources affect people in different ways. But, I have noticed that over the past number of years fewer of my students are challenging whether the Holodomor was a genocide.

3 December 2014

Ukrainian Journalist Wins International Press Freedom Award

http://hromadskeradio.org/2014/12/03/ukrainian-journalist-wins-international-press-freedom-award/
https://soundcloud.com/hromadske-radio/ukrainian-journalist-wins

Ukrainian journalist Oleksiy Matsiuka is this year's winner of the International Press Freedom Award. It's an award presented by the Canadian Journalists for Free Expression. For the past 17 years the organization has been seeking out and recognizing the work of a journalist who persists in working to find and share the news in difficult conditions. They host an Annual Gala, called "A Night to Honour Courageous Reporting", where they present the award. This year it's on 3 December at Toronto's landmark Fairmount Royal York Hotel.

Ukraine, or rather certain parts of it, where Russian-backed aggression has been going on for months, is certainly a dangerous place for journalists. Oleksiy had to flee his native city of Donets'k in April. His car was torched after he co-authored an article that linked separatist leaders to Moscow. Flyers with his photograph and the word "traitor" began appearing around the city. So, he now continues his investigative reporting from the capital, Kyiv.

CBC journalist Carol Off is the CJFE Gala Chair. This is what she had to say about the Ukrainian journalist: "Oleksiy doggedly reports on corruption, abuses of power and the conflict between Ukrainian and pro-Russian forces, despite ongoing threats and attacks. He outright refuses to be intimidated or silenced, and for this we're very proud to honour him with the 2014 IPFA."

Previous winners have included Egyptian Mohamed Abdelfattah (2011) and citizen journalist Rami Jarrah who covered the Syria story in 2012.

Oleksiy will meet with faculty and students at the University of Toronto's Center of European, Russian, and Eurasian Studies before receiving his award – thanks to the efforts of Professor Victor Ostapchuk.

15 December 2014

When Eyes Change: Look from a Different Angle

http://hromadskeradio.org/2014/12/15/when-eyes-change-look-from-a-different-angle-by-marta-dyczok/
https://soundcloud.com/hromadske-radio/when-eyes-change-look-from-a

The friendly eyes turned hard.

"Crimea is Russia. It has always been Russian", said the tall blond woman in stylish boots.

A minute ago we were discussing technology – how it affects classroom teaching. I had just finished complimenting her salad that we were enjoying at a reception after a seminar about slavery and citizenship in 19th century Brazil.

Conversation came to a lull, so I asked, "has anyone been following the news?" Russian President Putin gave his state of the nation address where he said that Crimea was an integral part of Russia, and the US House of Representatives adopted a statement condemning Russia's incursion into Ukraine and other neighboring states.

That's when the eyes changed.

The Russian student studying in Canada for years, making nice salads for receptions, spoke up and began defending Putin, attacking the US.

I was shocked. 'Wow,' was the first thing that came out of my mouth.

"You know that Russia annexed Crimea, and has troops in Eastern Ukraine," or something like that, followed.

"There was a referendum, that's what people wanted," she replied.

"Referendum at the barrel of a machine gun?" I asked.

The conversation became a bit heated. Another student joined in and began criticizing US policy in Iraq, the Middle East, Israel.

"But how does that legitimize Russia violating international law and annexing the territory of a neighboring state?" I asked.

That's when the student from Russia said that Crimea was Russia, and Russia had just given it to Ukraine in 1956.

"1954, actually," I heard myself correcting her, "and it was Khrushchev, Secretary General of the USSR." and started explaining what had been going on in Ukraine over the past year, and how information was being used as a weapon to distort things.

The seminar coordinator, who studies migration, was visibly uncomfortable. She tried to diffuse the tension with, "coffee, anyone?"

Taking her cue, I turned to the speaker and shifted conversation to her research interests, asked what she was planning. She spoke about her next speaking engagements, how she was using them to visit family and friends around the world.

Then she politely asked about my research. I told her that I study mass media, how narratives are constructed, and how they influence public opinion. That gave me an opening to ask the Russian student where she looked for information on news about Russia. She was honest and said Russian media. "You realize you're repeating Putin's narrative," I said.

I'm not sure that anything I said really convinced her. She seemed pretty firm in her views about Russia, that what Putin is doing is legitimate.

But as I was leaving I suggested that we try and see things as they are. The Russian student said, "maybe I should look at some other sources of information." the hardened eyes seemed to soften, a fraction.

13 January 2015

Non-Lethal Military Aid from Canada: No Pay on Delivery

http://hromadskeradio.org/2015/01/13/canada-ukraine-no-pay-on-delivery-marta-dyczok-on-another-shipment-of-non-lethal-military-aid/
https://soundcloud.com/hromadske-radio/canada-ukraine-no-pay-on

42 containers of non-lethal military aid from Canada arrived in Odessa on the third day of Ukrainian Christmas. Communications systems, medical kits, night vision goggles and military clothing.

It's the latest in a series of shipments. A previous one had arrived in Boryspil Airport on the 28th of November of last year. That was two days after Canadian Defense Minister Rob Nicholson announced an additional $11 million of aid.

I'm not sure whether other countries have sent such aid to Ukraine. The US announced a $53 million package of non-lethal aid last September. But I haven't seen any reports of it arriving. Perhaps the Americans are just not advertising their assistance. Unlike Canadians. The Ukrainian Canadian Congress even worked with #BABYLON 13 and produced a short film about the November shipment.
https://www.youtube.com/watch?v=I5-fHMa3Kkk#t=244

Like last time, the January Canadian shipment was met by volunteers from both Canada and Ukraine. They were there to assist government officials from both sides.

"Now the real work begins," Lenna Koszarny said on FB from Odessa. The Canadian-Ukrainian businesswoman chairs the UCC Ukraine Advisory Council. She was smiling as she met with the other volunteers to inspect the containers. Some of the containers were blue and yellow.

Mykola is a soldier I stay in touch with. He's fighting in the Donbas and recently posted photos of Canadian Forces winter gear. With a request. He asked anyone seeing them for sale to report the blackmarketeers. As I hear reports that fighting is intensifying, I'm hoping to see photos of Mykola with some of that Canadian aid soon, delivered by government officials and volunteers.

9 February 2015

Ukraine Again the Focus of International Attention

http://hromadskeradio.org/2015/02/09/ukraine-again-the-focus-of-international-attention-marta-dyczok-on-media-coverage-of-the-crisis/

Ukraine was all over the news the past few days. A flurry of high level diplomatic meetings in Kyiv, Moscow, Munich, and a series of phone calls between key international leaders focused the world's attention on the war in Ukraine. In a way that 31 civilians killed in Mariupol on 24 January did not.

Much of the reporting was about the possibility of the US supplying Ukraine with lethal weapons. Many experts were consulted, and opinion was divided. Relatively few western media outlets asked experts from Ukraine to comment. Some treated Ukraine as an object rather than a subject of international affairs.

American International Relations professor John Mearsheimer had an opinion piece in the New York Times on 8 February. He wrote, "What advocates of arming Ukraine fail to understand is that Russian leaders believe their country's core strategic interests are at stake in Ukraine… Great powers react harshly when distant rivals project military power into their neighbourhood."

Russian foreign minister Sergey Lavrov's speech at the Munich Security Conference was widely reported. Including the fact that the audience laughed when he said, "What happened in Crimea was the people invoking the right of self-determination. You've got the read the UN Charter. Territorial integrity and sovereignty must be respected."

Last March the media treated Lavrov as a respected commentator on events in Crimea.

16 March 2015

Consider Reconsidering: Reflections on Ukraine's Story in the Media

http://hromadskeradio.org/2015/03/16/consider-reconsidering-marta-dyczok-s-reflections-on-ukraine-s-story-in-media/

'The taxi driver was repeating Putin's narrative!' Vlad told me. The Ukrainian historian was in disbelief. He was on his way to the airport in Edmonton, in Canada – a country where information on current affairs is readily available.

But international public opinion on Ukraine is divided, in part because of the way mass media has been representing the story. Rules of objective reporting require that all sides must be given voice. So, Russian President Putin's statements were reported – as well as those of US President Obama, Ukrainian President Poroshenko, German Chancellor Merkel and others. In a situation where information is being used as a weapon, this has worked against the goal of media providing accurate coverage, a clear picture of events in Ukraine, their causes, and consequences.

Each person interprets news reports through the prism of their own value systems and beliefs. So, those who hold anti-American views because of US policy in the Middle East respond positively to Putin's criticism of Obama and statements that the U.S. was behind the Euromaidan protests and is fueling war in Ukraine to weaken Russia.

The Edmonton taxi driver was looking at Ukraine through his negative attitude towards the U.S. until he picked up a Ukrainian historian who filled in the picture for him on the way to the airport. "I think I convinced him to reconsider his perspective", Vlad said.

10 April 2015

Was the Pianist Doing the Best She Could?

http://hromadskeradio.org/2015/04/10/was-the-pianist-doing-the-best-she-could-marta-dyczok-reports-from-toronto/

Toronto's Symphony Orchestra dropped a pianist from their program. It was brought to their attention that Valentyna Lisitsa, a talented Ukrainian-born pianist, had been posting offensive tweets. She compared Ukrainian leaders to Nazis. Called Ukrainians dog feces. Juxtaposed photos of Ukrainian teachers wearing traditional embroidered shirts with Africans performing a dance with the comment: "teachers forced to wear Ukrainian tribal dress, a truly European custom :)" Posted a photo of pig testicles painted blue and yellow and wrote "Here are the faces of the leaders."

When she was removed from the TSO program a social media campaign was launched. Canada's most prestigious symphony orchestra was accused of censorship and the story hit the headlines. I noticed it, but initially didn't pay too much attention, because it was the end of term and my Easter was coming. But, as a lover of classical music and media watcher I couldn't but help follow the story.

Free speech was the topic of my last class on media and politics. My students debated the age old question of how and where to draw the line between free speech and hate speech. Is it acceptable to allow deliberately offensive statements and images in the public sphere? Who decides? And what criteria are used?

Canada's Criminal Code prohibits hate propaganda in sections 318, 319, and 320 of the Criminal Code. But few cases have been brought to court, even fewer successfully prosecuted. And social media is still somewhat in a grey zone when it comes to legislation.

When asked about her offensive tweets on CBC radio, Lisitsa said, "It's satirical. There's great space for exaggeration and hyperbole."

TSO president and CEO Jeff Melanson said that, "Free speech is important, but when it's offensive and hurtful, that's another matter." They conducted an investigation into the tweets, and asked the pianist to explain. "She had originally led us to believe that these might be someone else's words," Melanson said in an interview, but later she confirmed that the words were indeed hers. "We did not go public with this story because we were trying to protect Valentina and her reputation. We are now going public because she basically forced the issue on us and now we are speaking to you." And he released a full list of the tweets they investigated.

https://dl.dropboxusercontent.com/u/61455732/Lisitsa_Social_Media_Posts.pdf
(PDF Password: "*MusicalToronto*")

They hired Toronto born pianist Stewart Goodyear to play the scheduled concert. But that got cancelled too, after what Goodyear described as 'mob-like behavior' of Lisitsa's supporters. "I was accused of supporting censorship, and bullied into declining this engagement," he wrote on his Facebook page.

Media coverage has been mixed. Some accuse the orchestra of censorship. Others, like the Globe and Mail's Kate Taylor wrote, '"I'd expect to be fired if I used images of either Holocaust victims or African dancers in almost any satirical context."

Even though the TSO asked Lisitsa not to perform, they honored the contract from a financial perspective. They will pay her even, though she will not be playing.

When the TSO cancelled Lisitsa's performance, she offered a free solo concert to a downtown Toronto church. The church opted out.

22 April 2015

Interview with Serhii Plokhii

http://hromadskeradio.org/programs/various/scholar-reframes-vision-of-cold-wars-end-serhii-plokhy-interviewed-by-marta-dyczok

Harvard Professor Serhii Plohkii is this year's winner of the prestigious Lionel Gelber Prize for the world's best non-fiction book in English on foreign affairs, for *The Last Empire: The Final Days of the Soviet Union* (Oneworld Publications 2015). He holds the Mykhailo Hrushevs'kyi Chair of Ukrainian History at Harvard University and is also Director of the Harvard Ukrainian Research Institute. He flew to Toronto to receive his award and found time to give an interview to Hromadske Radio.

Marta Dyczok: In this award winning book you completely reframe our vision of the end of the Cold War and the last days of the Soviet Union by moving away from the American triumphalist narrative and focus on tensions between Gorbachev and Yelstin – and propose that the relationship between Ukraine and Russia and events in Ukraine and the Republics were perhaps more important, or as important, in the collapse of the Soviet Union. To what degree do the events of 1991 cast a shadow, or perhaps help us understand what's been happening in Ukraine in the years 2013-2014?

Serhii Plokhii: I'm moving from the mythology of the end of the Cold War that is present not only in the United States but also in Russia, because it's the same myth about America wiping the Soviet Union off the map of the world that is shared by many in Washington and in Moscow. Except that in Washington this is treated as a positive thing and in Moscow this is the source of resentment. In President Putin's speech on the annexation of the Crimea in March 2014 he was directly referring to the humiliation of 1991 and the alleged robbery of Russia as a result of the disintegration of the Soviet Union. So in that sense I'm trying to work against this dominant narrative both in the United States and in Russia.

By focusing on Ukraine and Russia instead of Washington and Bush and Gorbachev, what we get is actually a better perspective on the fall of the Soviet Union. Because a lot of what was happening was happening in the relations between the Republics. And second, we get a better perspective on relations between Russia and Ukraine. And a lot of issues, a lot of problems that came to the fore in the course of the last year, they were already there, the seeds of them were already there, back in 1991. It was in late August of 1991 that the spokesman for the Russian President Yeltsin, Pavel Vashchanov, first voiced these claims – Russian claims for Crimea, for eastern Ukraine, the Donets'k region in particular and also to some regions of Kazakhstan. It was also in the fall of 1991 that the decision was made in Moscow, around Yeltsin, that the empire, in the form that it had existed, in the form of the Soviet Union, was too expensive an enterprise for Russia, that Russia should focus on itself, use its oil and gas resources to rebuild itself and then, it was said, that the Republics would come back one way or another, twenty years later. And from that point of view, what is happening today is not just an invention of Mr. Putin but we see the roots of that kind of thinking in the entourage of President Yeltsin as early as 1991.

Marta Dyczok: Regarding the title of your book, *The Last Empire: The Final Days of the Soviet Union*. Some people have been commenting that the behavior of Russian President Putin is imperialist, or neo-imperialist. Was it really the last empire? Or is this just a new form of empire that we're seeing?

Serhii Plokhii: What I do in the book is I explain what I mean when I use the term empire, because there are many ways of using this term, its broad enough. And what I say is that I look at the Soviet Union as the last classic empire of the modern era of the 18th, 19th and 20th centuries, and put the collapse of the Soviet Union into the context of the disintegration of other empires, starting with Austria-Hungary, the Ottoman Empire, the French Empire, the British Empire, the Portuguese Empire. And from that point of view it transformed itself in the form of the Soviet Union but it was a continuation of that classic empire of the 18th and 19th century.

What we see now is not really an attempt to re-create the Soviet Union, not an attempt to recreate the Russian Empire on the part of Putin. Russia is looking for a more effective and cheaper way of dominating the area and dominating the space, through using, of course, its military, but also through using its culture, and language, and through using economic power, economic muscle, that it has. So in terms of the classic empire, it's kind of a post-imperial mode of behavior, but again, Russia is not the only country that has been trying to do that, it didn't invent that. But that's already a different understanding of imperialism than the one that existed in the 19th and 20th

centuries.

Marta Dyczok: Every empire needs some sort of legitimization, a narrative, a historical myth. What is the role of history, historical memory, the historian, in the construction of this new identity, this new empire, or if you will neo-empire, that the Russian president is promoting? What is the role of the historian here?

Serhii Plokhii: The role of the historian first of all is to look beyond the discourse that exists today, to look really what the New Russia or Novorossiya meant, what the declaration of the Donets'k Republic in 1917-1918 really meant. But the role of the historian is also to understand the roots, and in the roots maybe we will be able to better understand today, and maybe tomorrow as well.

When I look at the discourse used today by Russia in this Russian-Ukrainian really war today, the roots go back to the Imperial Russia of pre-1917. New Russia, *Novorossiya*, is just one of many examples of that. But it's also the emphasis on language, culture, and religion, emphasis on Orthodoxy, that's something that certainly didn't exist during Soviet times. And it's the denial, on a certain level, the right of the Ukrainians, or little Russians, or Belarussians, to exist as a separate nation, something that was characteristic of the official Russian discourse before 1917. And it is coming back. If the Soviet experiment, or the Soviet nationality policy at least rhetorically recognized Ukrainians and Belarussians as separate nations, now Putin repeats again and again that as far as he is concerned, Russians and Ukrainians constitute the same people. And this is really hearkening back to, going back to the official imperial discourse before 1917. So understanding, looking at the *longue durée* process, going beyond the headlines in the newspapers, this is the role of the historian but also of intellectuals in general in today's society, the way to contribute towards resolving the current crisis.

Marta Dyczok: Thank you for your contribution, and congratulations on your award!

29 April 2015

Ukrainian Frontline Song Comes to Toronto on Relief Weekend

http://hromadskeradio.org/2015/04/29/ukrainian-frontline-song-comes-to-toronto-on-relief-weekend-marta-dyczok-reports/

I finally got to see Foma perform live! The front man of Ukraine's famous folk-rock, blues, ska group Mandry was the headliner at a benefit concert for Ukraine in Toronto, organized by the NGO Dopomoha Ukraini. The concert was part of an event called, "A Weekend for Ukraine: Rock, Reforms & Relief". Proceeds are going to Patriot Defence, and the ATO Widows Rehabilitation Program. The evening also featured Michael Shchur and the Lemon Bucket Orkestra.

Last minute addition Yana Bilyk turned out to be a friend of the friend I went to the concert with. We went early since I had to pick up my ticket at the door, so I got to sit in the front row. And saw Foma do his sound check.

John Moskalyk, one of the organizers, acted as the MC. He opened the evening with a big thank you to the performers and the audience. The house was full. John even worried that there may be more people in the room than fire regulations allowed. Kids, seniors, teens, and the middle age crowd mingled comfortably.

The most powerful part of the concert for me was when Foma sang Hrady Vohniani, (Fiery Hrad Rockets). It's a song he recently composed while visiting the war zone, where Ukrainians regularly face incoming fire from Hrad rocket launchers. Hrad means hail. Before singing it, he told the audience that volunteers and soldiers he'd met said they listen to the song at the front.

But always the performer, Foma then moved to a more upbeat note and soon had people not only moving to the music in their seats but standing up and dancing. His energy touched me and, as he danced and sang on the stage, I found myself rising from my seat and joining in. A colleague from another university drifted over and began spinning me across the improvised dance floor.

"And now for the last song, it's a slow one," Foma said, or something like that. But after the 'last song' the audience asked for more. So Foma obliged. A few times.

Finally, he said, "I think you all know the words to this last, last song." And began singing Ukraine's national anthem. He changed the first few words to "Є і буде Україна," (Ukraine exists, and it always will.) Of course, the audience joined in.

26 May 2015

A Declaration of Identity. A Ukrainian Tradition

http://hromadskeradio.org/2015/05/26/a-declaration-of-identity-a-ukrainian-tradition-by-marta-dyczok-toronto/

Ukrainian embroidered shirts are both old and new. International designers like Dolce & Gabbana and Valentino have taken Ukrainian national dress as the 'go to' trend in this spring's fashion.[7]

On May the 21st I saw many photos and videos of people all over the world wearing traditional Ukrainian shirts. It was Ukrainian embroidered shirt day.

According to one report, Ukrainians in China were the first to mark the celebration. Because of the time difference they donned their colorful shirts and carried Ukrainian flags hours before people in Ukraine woke up.[8]

On my way to the drugstore in Bloor West Village in Toronto, a young man walking with an elderly woman caught my eye. He was wearing an embroidered shirt as he casually strolled down the sunny street.

Later in the day I came across a video of the celebration in Mariupol. A city in the Donets'k oblast that had been taken over by anti-Ukrainian forces, then liberated and named the acting capital of the war-torn region. Watching people dancing in the center of the sunny coastal city, wearing embroidered

---

[7]   See here: http://www.theguardian.com/fashion/2015/apr/29/in-the-face-of-the-ongoing-conflict-ukrainian-fashion-is-having-a-moment

[8]   See here: http://vidia.org/2015/40454

shirts, I could hardly believe that mortar rockets were being fired at them just kilometers away.
https://m.youtube.com/watch?v=_Ztd2aXmVPs.

Some people told an interviewing journalist that they wore their Ukrainian shirts all the time. Others said they had put them on for the first time.
https://m.youtube.com/watch?v=MRqjlb6ysbc

Watching photos of Parliamentarians posing for the cameras in their embroidered shirts I thought about Levko Lukianenko. He wore his embroidered shirt in Parliament in 1991, when no one else did, because it wasn't trendy. He'd spent 27 years in the Soviet Gulag. I guess the shirt was a sort of armor for him – a declaration of identity that could not be erased but needed to be demonstrated.

My family was displaced from Ukraine by World War II. None of the old embroidered shirts survived. My mother embroidered, so I grew up with new ones. But have always loved the old, and smile when I see a friend wearing a shirt from an ancestor.

On Ukrainian embroidered shirt day I wore something old/new. It's an antique embroidery I bought in Ukraine's capital, Kyiv that has an unusual cut. Created a long time ago but new to me. It made me feel connected to the spirit of the day, as well as the past.

9 June 2015

Cautious Because of Allies? Harper's Visit to Ukraine

http://hromadskeradio.org/2015/06/09/cautious-because-of-allies-marta-dyczok-on-canada-s-pm-visit-to-ukraine-from-kyiv/

Canadian Prime Minister Stephen Harper stopped in Kyiv on the 6th of June, on his way to the G7 summit in Germany. He met with Ukrainian President Poroshenko, Prime Minister Yatseniuk, visited a police academy and announced an additional 5 million dollars in aid to reform Ukraine's security sector. That day, Harper's visit to Ukraine was the lead story in many Canadian media outlets.

When Harper arrived in Germany for the summit, Canadian headlines read: "Ukraine conflict dominates G7 Summit", and "Harper uses G7 summit to push for Canada-EU free trade agreement."

Canada has been a staunch supporter of Ukraine for the past year and a half. Harper has visited Kyiv three times. In March 2014, he strongly condemned the annexation of Crimea. In June 2014 he was the only G7 leader to attend President Poroshenko's inauguration. A year later he visited again, before going to Germany. But when Ukrainian leaders asked for military support, the Canadian leader was cautious. He highlighted the non-lethal military equipment Canada has been sending. But beyond that, Harper said that Canada has to act in concert with its allies and that the matter was "the subject of ongoing dialogue".

24 June 2015

Two Oaths a Year Apart

http://hromadskeradio.org/node/20718

A year ago I watched a young man take an oath to protect Ukraine and head out to the front in the ranks of the Battalion Donbas. Last week I watched the same young man, who survived the battle of Ilovais'k and being taken prisoner. He was taking an oath to his sweetheart in a wedding ceremony in Odessa.

What struck me most were his eyes. They were as bright and strong as the day I met him, on 23 June 2014, before he went into war. Along with 479 other volunteers, Sashko was taking his military oath at the Interior Ministry base just outside of Nova Petrivka near Kyiv. We spoke only briefly. He told me that he was from the Odessa oblast, that he'd turned 21 that day, had 3 weeks of training, and was going to defend his country. His mother asked me not to post the photos I took anywhere. So I just e-mailed them to his brother, who was there sending him off.

We stayed in touch. Over the course of the year I heard about what Sashko went through from his brother. A lot of it made me cry. And, then came the wedding invitation and I couldn't stop smiling.

After the ceremony his mother told me that when Sashko returned from his first tour of duty, his eyes were dark. But, then she noticed that he developed a new determination for life.

In the fall Sashko hopes to resume his law studies at the university. After graduating he wants to be a prosecutor. I can't wait to see that.

7 August 2015

Millet, Vatan, Qirim. Nation, Homeland, Crimea: Crimean Tatar's World Congress in Ankara

http://hromadskeradio.org/en/krimski-hroniki/millet-vatan-qirim-nation-homeland-crimea

"We will never give up" said Refat Chubarov. The Crimean Tatar leader was addressing his people. They'd come from all over the world to participate in the Second Crimean Tatar Congress held in Ankara, Turkey, on the 1st and 2nd of August 2015. "No one can determine the destiny of Crimea without the Crimean Tatar people," he continued. "We have lived there for a 1,000 years." Delegates rose to their feet and began chanting, "nation, homeland, Crimea."

It was really interesting to watch 430 delegates from 14 countries representing 184 Crimean Tatar organizations meet and debate priorities, policies, procedures, in their own language.

Seventy-seven-year-old former dissident Ayshe Seyturmatova came from Simferopol. Khalil Khalilov recently completed a commerce degree at the Rotman School and flew in from Toronto. A round faced man in fatigues with Genghis Khan as his 'nom de guerre' arrived from the war zone in the Donbas.

Along with the others, over two days they restructured the international organization – the Congress – so that the Crimean Tatar people can speak with one voice and make it more effectively heard internationally. Mejlis leader Refat Chubarov has been banned from Crimea for five years, but they elected him to head the Congress.

The event was funded by Turkey and criticized by Russia. Crimean Tatar leaders from Crimea were prevented from participating by those currently controlling the peninsula. Ukraine's Foreign Minister Pavlo Klimkin attended as well as Turkish politicians and a variety of diplomats.

Crimea's parliament dismissed the event as a fringe effort. But, Turkey's president Recep Erdogan met with the Crimean Tatar Congress leadership as soon as he returned from China.

And 'Genghis Khan' invited me to his native Yevpatoria for plov as soon as what he calls the second Russian occupation is over, and he can return.

Conclusion

Revolution, annexation, war, and economic crisis are not ideal conditions for independent media to operate in. But, that's the reality Ukraine found itself in after the Euromaidan protests of 2013-2014 – and society needed accurate information and objective analysis more than ever.

The years 2014-2016 were challenging for all Ukrainians, including journalists. When the difficult and deadly domestic protests ended, the country found itself on the receiving end of a hybrid war coming from Russia. Part of the Kremlin's strategy was weaponizing information and the term 'information war' gained entirely new dimensions. Journalists faced new threats. State censorship within Ukraine largely ended, but journalists faced new risks to their physical safety and lives. Initial unity and enthusiasm for change in the media sphere gradually got bogged down, and many began wondering had anything changed? One bright spot on the complex new landscape was Hromadske Radio (Public Radio Ukraine), which produced ever more quality programing.

On 22 February 2014 the Ukrainians, who had protested for months, felt they had won when corrupt president Victor Yanukovych fled the country. After standing through the cold and snow these people felt that they had gained a new chance to reform their country and continue on the road to membership of the European Union.

Victory had come at a high price. Protesters and journalists had been beaten. Over 100 were killed. Ukrainians buried their dead, selected an interim president and government, set a date for new elections and looked forward. Although not all Ukrainians supported the protests, the drama of those events caught the world's imagination. A film about them later received an Oscar nomination.[9] But, at the time, few could have anticipated that within days Ukraine would face a new, deadlier, threat that would cost thousands of lives and displace millions from their homes.

---

[9] Winter on Fire: Ukraine's Fight for Freedom, directed by Evgeny Afineevsky, 2015, http://www.imdb.com/title/tt4908644/ and http://oscar.go.com/news/nominations/winter-on-fire-ukraines-fight-for-freedom-gets-best-documentary-feature-film-oscar-nomination-2016

On 26 February 2014 heavily armed masked soldiers with no insignia on their uniforms began taking over government buildings in Crimea. They surrounded military bases and mass media outlets. It gradually became clear that these were Russian troops. The soldiers ousted Crimea's elected legislature, installed a new government, organized an event they called a 'referendum', and announced that over 95% of the population voted to join Russia. By 16 March 2016, Russia's annexation of Crimea was complete.

Around the same time, violence began in eastern regions of Ukraine that bordered Russia. Crowds stormed government buildings, took them over, and hoisted Russian flags. Who were in the crowds? According to eye-witnesses and later investigations, it was a combination of local Ukrainians, people brought in from elsewhere (presumably Russia) and Russian special operatives. One key figure was Igor Girkin, a Russian military and intelligence officer, who took the *nom du guerre* Igor Strelkov, and had participated in the Crimean events before moving to Donets'k.

Ukrainian security services were slow to respond, in part because many of them had been penetrated by Russian operatives and were not loyal to their own state. So, ordinary Ukrainians began organizing voluntary battalions and pushing back.[10] Things escalated. And within months a hybrid war had erupted in the Donets'k and Luhans'k regions. Parts of both provinces came under control of anti-Ukrainian forces who set up entities they called the Donets'k and Luhans'k People's Republics (DNR and LNR). The first Prime Minister of the DNR was a Muscovite called Alexandr Borodai.[11]

The phrase 'information war' started to proliferate when the struggle for accurate information became a key part of the larger conflict. Russian media and government sources launched a sophisticated operation sending out mixed messages, half-truths, and deliberate distortions aimed at clouding the picture of what was really going on. Initially they denied being in Crimea. Then, the story changed. Russia admitted to sending troops there, but to protect ethnic Russians from Ukrainian right wing fascists.

All pro-Ukrainians were labeled fascists – including the new President Poroshenko. While it was true that there had been extreme right wing elements in the Euromaidan protests, they were a small fringe and were not

---

[10] Here is a short report about one of these volunteers for PRU: 24 June 2015, Two Oaths a Year Apart. Marta Dyczok from Odessa Region on a Soldier's Wedding. http://hromadskeradio.org/node/20718. Some of the volunteer battalions were made up of nationalists, which added fuel to the Kremlin's information war.

[11] See http://www.bbc.com/news/world-latin-america-27211501

in the interim or later elected government. The narrative about eastern Ukraine presented in Russian media was that pro-Russian separatists were rising up against an illegitimate fascist government in Kyiv that had seized power through an illegal coup – and that they wanted to join Russia too. Even after the 25 May 2014 presidential election, Russia continued to call Ukraine's government illegitimate.

The Kremlin deliberately and skillfully chose terminology and imagery that drew on the Soviet era glorification the Red Army's defeat of the bloodthirsty fascists and demonization of the Ukrainian nationalist movement led by Stepan Bandera. Labeling people fascists and banderites evoked powerful negative emotional responses among people who were lukewarm towards the Ukrainian government. The larger goal of the information war was to delegitimize Ukrainian authorities, cause panic and instability, and present Russia as a desirable alternative.

Blatantly untrue stories, aimed at fostering anti-Ukrainian sentiment, became a regular feature in Russian media that was as easily available in Ukraine as US media is available in Canada. One such example was the 12 July 2014 interview with a supposed refugee from Slavians'k, where Ukrainian forces had pushed back the DNR forces. Russian TV channel ORT aired an interview with a woman who identified herself as Galina who said that she's witnessed a public execution and crucifixion of a 3-year-old boy by Ukrainian soldiers. Western and Ukrainian journalists soon exposed that the story had been entirely fabricated – but people who only consult Russian media may continue to believe the story to be true.[12]

How did Ukraine's media respond to these events? It would be fair to say the reaction was mixed, and changed over time.

When President Yanukovych disappeared, state pressures on media disappeared too. The immediate reaction was that more comprehensive, balanced and objective information began appearing in Ukraine's media space. Investigative journalism enjoyed a brief revival. Most major media outlets began asking questions about what had happened during the Euromaidan protests. Why had so many people been killed? Who did the shooting? Who gave the orders? Who is investigating? These became common questions in the public sphere.

---

[12] http://www.wsj.com/articles/arkady-ostrovsky-putins-ukraine-unreality-show-1406590397
and https://www.youtube.com/watch?v=Xf8Gt2Wnv74

When the Russian invasion began, all major Ukrainian television channels began programing aimed at national unity. A new logo appeared on all their screens that read, "A United Country," in both Ukrainian and Russian. They also all agreed not to air Russian-produced entertainment programming that glorified the Russian Army or their Special Forces, or even the Soviet Red Army. The privately owned Channel 1+1 created an English language station which they called *Ukraine Today*. Its aim was to provide information from within Ukraine to the outside world and was launched on 14 August 2014.

Before that, Hromadske Radio was on the front lines seeking out and reporting on events in English whenever they could. Reporter Andriy Kulykov travelled to Perevalnie in Crimea on 5 March 2015, from where he sent a dispatch he titled, "'Unknown Soldier' Acquires New Meaning in Crimea".[13] Two weeks later he was in Donets'k, reporting how masked men carrying submachine guns came to the Donbas TV station,[14] and later how a crowd in the city center was shouting "Rossia!"[15]

Violence and war changed life for all Ukrainians, but it changed for journalists in a specific way. Issues of journalistic standards, ethics, censorship, self-censorship, and propaganda moved beyond conferences and round table discussions. They became linked to matters of national security, and in many cases, personal security. The phrase 'information war' became so widely used because the struggle for accurate information became a key part of the larger conflict.

Heavily armed masked men perpetrating violence didn't want the world to see what they were doing. So they targeted journalists, kidnapped, tortured, and even killed them.[16] 2014 became the deadliest year for journalists in Ukraine's modern history. Seven were killed, 25 arrested, 79 kidnapped or detained, 286 assaulted. Journalist/fixer Maria Varfolomeyeva spent over a year under arbitrary detention by the self-proclaimed Luhans'k People's Republic before

---

[13] Andriy Kulykov reporting from Pereval'ne in Crimea 5 March 2014, "Unknown Soldier" Acquires New Meaning in Crimea, https://soundcloud.com/hromadske-radio/unknkown-soldier-acquires-new

[14] Donbas TV Channel: Working Amid Trouble. Andriy Kulykov Reports from Donets'k. 11 March 2015, https://soundcloud.com/hromadske-radio/donbas-tv-channel-working-amid

[15] "Russia," The Battle Cry of March 16. Andriy Kulykov Reports from Donets'k, 16 March 2015, https://soundcloud.com/hromadske-radio/russia-the-battle-cry-of-march

[16] For example see, Marta Dyczok, "Masked Men vs. Journalists in Ukraine," Wall Street Journal, 29 April 2014, http://www.wsj.com/articles/SB10001424052702304393704579528101344061812

being released on 3 March 2016.[17]

The majority of incidents occurred in Kyiv in the last days of the Euromaidan protests – in Crimea, and the eastern areas where war broke out. That year, Ukraine was named one of the three most dangerous countries in the world for journalists.[18]

Needless to say, most journalists were unprepared for what they were facing. There wasn't a tradition of war journalism in Ukraine, much less of a war being fought on their own territory. Some had to flee their homes. Others headed out into the conflict zone without any training or proper equipment like helmets or bullet proof vests. Others lost sight of objectivity and took sides.

Ukrainian and international reporting of these events was uneven for many reasons. In some cases, comprehensive information was difficult (if not impossible) to obtain because access in the war zone was restricted by all sides. Many journalists in Crimea and areas of Donbas that came under control of the self-proclaimed Donets'k and Luhans'k People's Republics were detained. Others fled for their safety to areas controlled by Ukrainian authorities. For example, Serhii Harmash, Editor of the independent Donets'k on-line publication, *Ostrov*, had survived the Kuchma and Yanukovych era censorship but had to flee when his editorial office was shot at in March 2014. Ukrainian television and radio were taken off the air, as was the independent Crimean Tatar TV station ATR.[19]

There were also issues of terminology and effectiveness. Russia was denying any involvement, calling events "referenda" and "civil war" in Ukraine. It did a very good job of getting its message out to international media outlets in the early months of the conflict. For their part, the new Ukrainian authorities called their actions an "Anti-Terrorist Operation" (ATO) rather than a war, and initially did not do a very good job of getting their message out to their own citizens or the international community.

Ukrainian civil society stepped up. In March 2014 a group of PR experts created the Ukraine Crisis Media Center (UCMC) which they envisioned as a

---

[17] See here: http://www.unian.info/society/1281764-journalist-maria-varfolomeeva-freed-from-militant-captivity.html#ad-image-0
[18] Data collected by the Institute of Mass Information in Ukraine, http://imi.org.ua/en/, used in the Freedom House Report on Freedom of the Press, https://freedomhouse.org/report/freedom-press/freedom-press-2015#.VqPn5oUrLIV
[19] They continue to be available online.

temporary platform where government officials could meet with journalists and provide information. It became the place where the spokesperson for Ukraine's ATO operation, colonel Andriy Lysenko, gave daily press briefings. "In face of what was going on, we put our careers on hold and created this center," co-founder Natalya Popovych said. "At the time, we thought it would be only for a few weeks."[20] Although Ukrainian state efforts in the information war improved, the UCMC continued to exist two years later.

A group of journalists and scholars set up a project called StopFake, in which they monitored fake news about Ukraine coming from the Kremlin and setting the record straight. After Petro Poroshenko was elected president on 25 May 2015, the government information services (press bureaus) gradually began to work more effectively. However, the grass roots initiatives continued to exist and play an important role.

Two controversial state moves were introduced after Poroshenko became president. Russian television and radio broadcasts into Ukraine were banned and the Ministry of Information Policy was created. The decision to take Russian media off the air in Ukraine came in the summer of 2014. This came after Ukrainian television was taken off the air in Russian controlled Crimea and the parts of Donets'k and Luhans'k that came under control of the self-proclaimed Donets'k and Luhans'k Peoples Republics. The decision was taken by the National Council on TV and Radio Broadcasting, the state regulatory agency of the broadcast sphere. It was hotly debated and opposed by many journalists, but the justification given by the regulator was that Ukraine had to fight against the disinformation campaign by blocking. This was only partially successful, since Russian media is available on the internet or through satellite dishes.

Equally controversial was president Poroshenko's decision to create a Ministry of Information Policy in December 2014. The rationale presented at the time was that the state needed to coordinate information strategy in conditions of war. The new ministry was charged with the task of ensuring that accurate information was available both to Ukrainian society and the world, and to ensure that disinformation was challenged and corrected. A number of steps were taken by the Ministry. A document on Ukraine Information Security Concept was produced, which explained: "The main objective of the information security system is to sustain such development preventing negative impacts of third party interference."[21] A system of embedded journalism was introduced with the Ukrainian Armed Forces, and

---

[20] Interview with UCMC co-founder Nataliya Popvych, Kyiv, July 2014.
[21] See http://www.osce.org/node/175051

steps were taken to renew broadcasting in parts of Donbas. There was also an announcement that the Ministry would create a broadcaster to provide foreign language news about Ukraine internationally, and the platform was launched in October of 2015.[22] It was not clear whether the necessary financial resources for this venture would be forthcoming, or how it would significantly differ from the private English language TV channel *Ukraine Today*. Overall the Ministry faced much criticism and the Minister, Yuriy Stets, resigned after one year.

Perhaps the most important thing was that the structure of the media system remained basically unchanged. The large private media corporations that accounted for approximately 90% of the media landscape remained intact, with the same owners. Rinat Akhmetov, Ukraine's richest man who hails from Donets'k, largely disappeared from the public sphere once things heated up in the Donbas and his role in the events became a subject of public discussion. But, he remained the owner of Media Group Ukraine. Dmytro Firtash and Serhiy Lyovochkin, allies of the fugitive former President Yanukovych faced investigations for corruption in both Ukrainian and international courts, yet they reportedly continued to own INTER – Ukraine's largest media corporation. And, Petro Poroshenko, who became president in May 2015, refused to give up ownership of TV Channel 5.

Although right after the Euromaidan protests the private media corporations aired content aimed at promoting national unity, gradually they went back to reflecting and promoting the interests of their owners. This was especially visible during elections, when certain candidates and parties received excessive, or unfair, media coverage on these channels. A Ukrainian media content monitoring report issued in January 2016, almost two years after the Euromaidan revolution, concluded that the major TV channels had reverted to the same as they had been during the Yanukovych regime.[23]

Yet, there was one positive change. State owned media began transforming into public broadcasters – even if not as quickly as many would have liked. Things began enthusiastically in the spring of 2014 when the successful and charismatic journalist from Kharkiv, Zurab Alasaniya, was appointed director of the state TV company. He immediately began introducing changes. Censorship of the news ended right away. New programming was introduced, plans were made for a new management and regulatory structure of the

---

[22] See http://www.telekritika.ua/pravo/2015-06-24/108602
[23] Iryna Andreitsiv, "Stari Pisni Pro Holovne," [The Same old Song], *Media Sapiens*, 24 January 2016: http://osvita.mediasapiens.ua/monitoring/daily_news/stari_pisni_pro_golovne/

company. But, the process got bogged down in bureaucratic and legal issues. Two years later it was still incomplete. Alasaniya said numerous times, "I'll oversee this process and make sure Ukraine has public broadcasting even if it kills me."

Hromadske Radio has been part of the transition to public broadcasting, but in a different way. They worked bottom up rather than top down. They stuck to their original manifesto from the summer of 2013 to provide objective information to Ukrainian society and remain free from editorial interference, and they kept innovating. Right after the revolution they began talks with the state national radio company and in February 2014 received two daily prime time broadcast hours. They began airing a talk show they called 'The Community Wave' in addition to continuing their on-line podcasts. To support their efforts, they organized fundraising events, crowdfunding projects, applied for grants and invited donations through their website. Gradually they increased their staff, put in bids for tenders to gain airtime on FM frequencies, and increased their audience reach.

One area they targeted were the territories that were not controlled by Ukrainian government authorities. Their aim was to reach out to Ukrainians who had little access to Ukrainian information and were being barraged by Russian media. In the autumn of 2015 Hromadske Radio introduced a new live show called Kyiv-Donbas, which they produced in Russian – aiming to counteract the information war coming from Russia. By the autumn of 2015 they succeeded in winning public tenders to broadcast on local FM frequencies in the Donets'k and Luhans'k provinces.[24] On 1 February 2016 another new project was launched – a two-hour live morning talk show which they called 'The Morning Wave', broadcasted every day.

In all their programming they aim to maintain journalistic standards – for example using the phrase 'Ukrainian forces' rather than 'our troops' when reporting on the war. Being independent, they face two main challenges: they need to secure steady financing and navigate the complex relationship with the transforming national radio company. Retaining full editorial freedom while remaining part of the complex reform process with a state bureaucracy is no easy task. But, their vision is that in the future they will succeed in winning a tender for one of the three national frequencies owned by the company for their own programming.

---

[24] See http://hromadskeradio.org/en/2015/11/11/gromadske-radio-rozpochynaye-efirne-movlennya-na-donbasi

At the time of writing, they were exploring another new initiative. A regular English language program. They have invited me to participate in it.

Note on Indexing

E-IR's publications do not feature indexes due to the prohibitive costs of assembling them. However, if you are reading this book in paperback and want to find a particular word or phrase you can do so by downloading a free e-book version of this publication in PDF from the E-IR website.

When downloaded, open the PDF on your computer in any standard PDF reader such as Adobe Acrobat Reader (pc) or Preview (mac) and enter your search terms in the search box. You can then navigate through the search results and find what you are looking for. In practice, this method can prove much more targeted and effective than consulting an index.

If you are using apps such as iBooks or Kindle to read our e-books, you should also find word search functionality in those.

You can find all of our e-books at: http://www.e-ir.info/publications

www.ingramcontent.com/pod-product-compliance
Lightning Source LLC
Chambersburg PA
CBHW071008080526
44587CB00015B/2393